30 Day Whole Food Slow Cooker Challenge:

101 Irresistible Whole Food Slow Cooker Recipes That Will Help You Lose Weight, Prevent Disease, and Make You Feel Better Than Ever Before

VANESSA OLSEN

Copyright 2017 by Vanessa Olsen - All rights reserved.

This document is geared towards providing exact and reliable information in regards to the topic and issue covered. The publication is sold with the idea that the publisher is not required to render accounting, officially permitted, or otherwise, qualified services. If advice is necessary, legal or professional, a practiced individual in the profession should be ordered.

- From a Declaration of Principles which was accepted and approved equally by a Committee of the American Bar Association and a Committee of Publishers and Associations.

In no way is it legal to reproduce, duplicate, or transmit any part of this document in either electronic means or in printed format. Recording of this publication is strictly prohibited and any storage of this document is not allowed unless with written permission from the publisher. All rights reserved.

The information provided herein is stated to be truthful and consistent, in that any liability, in terms of inattention or otherwise, by any usage or abuse of any policies, processes, or directions contained within is the solitary and utter responsibility of the recipient reader. Under no circumstances will any legal responsibility or blame be held against the publisher for any reparation, damages, or monetary loss due to the information herein, either directly or indirectly.

Respective authors own all copyrights not held by the publisher.

The information herein is offered for informational purposes solely, and is universal as so. The presentation of the information is without contract or any type of guarantee assurance.

The trademarks that are used are without any consent, and the publication of the trademark is without permission or backing by the trademark owner. All trademarks and brands within this book are for clarifying purposes only and are the owned by the owners themselves, not affiliated with this document.

TABLE OF CONTENTS

Introduction xii
Chapter 1: The History of Slow Cooking 1
Chapter 2: Using a Slow Cooker 3
Chapter 3: Benefits of Slow Cooking 7
Chapter 4: Slow Cooking and a Whole Food Diet 11
Chapter 5: Whole-Food Pantry Staples 15
Chapter 6: A Month of Slow Cooker Whole Foods 19

Chapter 7 - Breakfast 23

    Breakfast Casserole 24
    Cauliflower-Sausage Breakfast Casserole 25
    Spinach + Feta Quiche 27
    Veggie Omelet 28
    Stuffed Peppers 30
    Ham + Spinach Frittata 31
    Breakfast Quinoa with Apple and Dates 33
    Blueberry + Peach Steel-Cut Oats 34
    Slow Cooker Granola 35
    Slow Cooker Yogurt 37

Chapter 8 - Poultry 39

Chicken with Tomatoes and Peppers 40
Easy Chicken Curry 42
Fiesta Chicken with Beans 44
Chicken Stew 45
Sweet 'n Sour Chicken 46
Garlic Rosemary Chicken + Potatoes................................ 48
Italian Sausage, Turkey, and Potatoes.............................. 49
Chicken with Fire-Roasted Tomatoes................................ 50
Chicken Chili... 51
Parmesan Garlic Chicken with Orzo and Vegetables......... 52
Chipotle Turkey Chili with Apples 54
Mediterranean-Spiced Roast Turkey 56

Chapter 9 - Beef.. 57

Spice-City Beef Taco Meat 58
10-Ingredient Beef Bourguignon.. 60
Italian Chuck Roast with Bell Peppers and Mushrooms 62
Steak Fajitas with Fixin's 64
Spicy Sloppy Joe's... 66
Ginger Beef... 68
Beef + Potato Au Gratin.. 70
Cinnamon-Kissed Pot Roast.. 72
Hoisin Beef Stew 74
Bean + Beef Chili 76

Orange-Spiced Corned Beef 77

Chapter 10 - Pork 79

Apple Cider Pork Roast 80
Pork Carnitas 82
Balsamic-Glazed Pork Loin 84
Parmesan Pork Roast 86
Chinese Five-Spice Pork Ribs 88
Dijon Pork Chops with Apples 90
Rustic Rosemary-Apple Pork Roast 91
Coconut Pork Curry 92
Ginger + Clove-Spiked Pulled Pork 94
Honey Mustard-Glazed Ham 96
Ham and Potatoes 97

Chapter 11 - Seafood 99

Mandarin-Orange Tilapia 100
Hearty Seafood Stew 101
Tilapia + Asparagus Packets 103
Tomato-Rosemary Cod 104
Asian Salmon Stir-Fry 106
Maple Salmon 107
Coconut-Milk White Fish 108
Shrimp Scampi 109
Shrimp Risotto 110

Seafood Gumbo ... 112

Tuna-Mushroom Casserole ... 114

Salmon Chowder ... 116

Clam Chowder ... 118

Chapter 12 - Sides + Snacks ... 120

Mashed Cauliflower with Garlic + Herbs ... 121

Garlic-Herb Mushrooms ... 123

Spiced Chickpeas ... 125

Beans + Rice ... 126

Macaroni and Cheese ... 127

Applesauce Sweet Potatoes ... 128

Creamed Corn ... 129

Butternut Squash with Apples and Cranberries ... 130

Rosemary-Honey Beets ... 131

Wild Rice Stuffing ... 133

Pear + Sausage Stuffing ... 135

Sweet Potato Casserole ... 137

Jalapeno Cornbread ... 139

Chapter 13 – Vegan ... 141

Carrot + Zucchini Cake Oatmeal ... 142

Perfect Vegetable Soup ... 143

Black Bean + Mango Chili ... 145

Butternut Squash + Bean Chili ... 147

Spaghetti Squash + Broccoli Bowl with Peanut Dressing 148
Lentil Stew with Polenta 150
Pineapple-Teriyaki Tofu 152
Braised Tofu 154
Spiced Potatoes + Chickpeas 156
Chocolate Pudding Cake 158
Green Apple Crumble 160

Chapter 14 - Dips and Sauces 161

Cheesy Crab Dip 162
Spinach Artichoke Dip 163
Chorizo-Chipotle Bean Dip 165
10-Hour Chicken Stock 167
Homemade Pizza Sauce 169
Vegetable Marinara Sauce 171
Garlic-Basil Tomato Sauce 173
Sausage + Beef Meat Sauce 174
Butternut Squash Sauce 176
Cranberry Sauce 178

Chapter 15 - Desserts 179

Cherry + Almond Dessert Oatmeal 180
Molten Lava Cake 181
Maple Créme Brûlée 183
Lemon Pudding Cake 185

Chai-Spiced Pears 187
Cranberry-Walnut Bread Pudding 188
Almond Banana Bread 190
Coconut Cream + Almond Butter-Stuffed Apples 192
Maple-Roasted Pear Crumble 194
Cocoa-Roasted Almonds 196

Conclusion 197

I would love to give you a gift. Please visit happyhealthycookingonline.com to get these 4 amazing eBooks for free!

Introduction

Slow cookers have been around for the good part of a century, but they're just as popular and effective as ever. Using one allows you to prep meals in the morning and cook them all day, or cook them overnight. The long, slow, and low cooking process creates deep, rich flavors and delicious meals everyone enjoys. This book introduces you to the slow cooker, from its history to operation to pros and cons. The heart of the informative chapters, however, is how slow cooking can be used to cook "whole foods." Eating whole foods is an organic, natural diet lifestyle that focuses on foods in their unprocessed, unrefined state. That means whole-grains, organic vegetables and fruit, and grass-fed meats. These foods are rich in fibers, minerals, and vitamins that are removed from the processed, packaged versions.

A whole food diet has a lot of benefits, including better resistance to disease, easier weight loss, more energy, better sleep, and more. A slow cooker is a great way to prepare meals from the whole foods you buy, and thanks to the low temperature, the nutrients lost from other cooking methods are preserved. The slow cooker is also really convenient, which is crucial when it comes to cooking healthy meals at home. If cooking isn't made easy, chances are you won't be able to stick to it for long. The last chapter in the first part of the book lists a bunch of pantry staples, most of which you'll find throughout the recipes. With a well-stocked pantry of whole foods, you'll always be able to make good choices and make every meal and snack count.

And what about the recipes? You'll find them divided up by sections like Breakfast, Poultry, Seafood, Sides + Snacks, Desserts, and so on. There are more than enough to build your new healthy whole-food menu whether you're cooking for one or twelve!

Chapter 1: The History of Slow Cooking

Slow cooking food is not a new concept, and certainly isn't one that can be credited to any one person. Lots of foods that have been around for centuries have historically been cooked slowly, especially stews. In fact, it was a stew that inspired the Crock-Pot, which was the first major commercially-produced slow cooker, and the name that most people call every slow cooker, regardless of its actual brand. Irving Naxon recalled a story from his grandmother about a Lithuanian stew called "cholent." The stew took hours, and involved leaving the food in an oven, going about the day, and returning home in the evening to finish the stew. Naxon acquired a patient in 1940, and released what he called "the Naxon Beanery" in the 1950's. In 1970, his company was bought by Rival, and they re-released the device as the now-famous Crock-Pot. It cost around $25.

In the 1970's, it became more common for women to have careers, so they wouldn't be at home all day and able to make meals. The Crock-Pot became a convenient way to start dinner in the morning before work, and then finish it when the day was over. However, because the Crock-Pot design was so focused on convenience, the meals it prepared weren't very good. Much of that can be blamed on the recipes available at the time - people just didn't know how to harness the slow cooker power correctly. That weakness didn't stop the slow cooker's popularity, and eager to catch up to the trends, other companies began releasing their own models. At one time, there were 40 companies making slow cookers.

By the 1980's, sales dipped a bit as the microwave became popular. However, the slow cooker has never suffered much, and in 2002, a study by Betty Crocker revealed that almost 81% of Americans still had a slow cooker. The enduring presence of the slow cooker can be credited to the many advances that have been embraced over the years. The first stride was the removable pot, so instead of coming in one clunky piece, a person could take out the pot to wash it. Better lids and tighter seals also helped turn the slow cooker into a portable addition to potlucks and other gatherings. In the age of smart technology, slow cookers are now equipped with programmable timers, one-touch cooking programs, and more.

Chapter 2: Using a Slow Cooker

Slow cookers have a relatively simple design that's shared by all the brands. It consists of the cooking pot, which can be inserted and removed from the housing. This housing, usually made of metal, holds the electrical heating element. The lid holds in the heat, but is not an air-tight seal, like with pressure cookers, so it can be removed at any time during cooking without turning off the cooker.

The slow cooker is operated by a control panel, which have advanced significantly since the Crock-Pot's inception. Most have at least two settings - high and low - while others also have a "medium" and "keep warm" setting. Advanced cookers can be programmed to start and end at a certain time, so you don't even have to be home to turn the cooker on and off.

What brands should you consider? Some of the best cookers in 2017 include the Crock-Pot Programmable Cooker, Cuisinart 3-In-1 Cook Central, and Black + Decker 7-Quart. Crock-Pot is a classic, so you know their cookers are going to be high-quality, while Cuisinart and Black + Decker are also giants in the food appliance industry. Price varies by size and technological advances. As an example, the Crock-Pot brand has a cooker with an app for your smartphone that lets you remotely control the time and temperature, so when you're not at home, you can still adjust your cooker as you need to. A slow cooker with that kind of tech costs upwards of $130.

In terms of size, some cookers are quite small at only 3.5 quarts, while larger ones are 6 or 7-quarts. Because you can safely fill a slow cooker pretty much right to the top, most families of four would be fine with 5-quart.

To use a slow cooker, you simply follow the instructions of a recipe and put all the food in the pot, close the lid, and go. Some recipes have you add certain ingredients later in the cooking process, because they don't take as long to cook. Most recipes also use some liquid, so the cooker can generate moisture and the food doesn't dry out. You'll notice as you read the recipes in this book that some do not have you add liquid. This either means the ingredients will generate their own liquid, or the recipe simply doesn't need it. When the cooker is on, the electrical heating element warms up the bottom and walls of the pot, providing a consistent, low temperature between 174-199 °F.

When a meal is finished, test the temperature to make sure whatever you've been cooking is at the appropriate temperature. To wash, simply remove the pot insert and wash by hand with a soft sponge or stick in your dishwasher. The inside of the lid can be wiped down quickly by hand, as well. To clean the exterior of your slow cooker, a paper towel and some warm water is usually all that's needed.

Troubleshooting common problems

Once you've been using your slow cooker for a while, you might notice some problems. Instead of chalking it up to your skills as a chef, here are some simple solutions to the most common issues:

Your meals are always really liquidy:

If you're adapting a recipe from a stovetop or oven, you can reduce the amount of liquid by 50%. If you're cooking meals like whole chickens or roasts, you can actually put in the meat without liquid, because the natural juices provide enough liquid. If you end up with a meal with more liquid than you want, just take off the lid and turn the slow cooker back on the highest setter for an hour. The excess moisture will evaporate.

Food is cooked unevenly:

It's pretty common for slow-cooked stews to have perfectly done meat with overcooked veggies. The solution is to always be sure to cut everything into equally-sized pieces, and add softer ingredients (vegetables especially) toward the end of the cooking time. Frozen veggies thaw quickly, so you can even add those after the slow cooking is done, and just stir till they are heated through.

Your cooker is smoking:

If your slow cooker begins smoking as soon as you turn it on, there's probably food or oil on the housing or the heating element itself. If your cooker is brand-new, it's probably just manufacturing oils burning off. After a few uses, the oil should be all gone, and the smoking should stop. If your cooker isn't new, make sure to clean up any food that's stuck to the cooker and burning when it heats up.

Chapter 3: Benefits of Slow Cooking

Convenience has always been the major selling point of the slow cooker, but there are other advantages that a home cook should be aware of, as well as some of the disadvantages. Here's what people love about the slow cooker:

Breaks down tough meats: Slow cooking turns even tougher, cheaper cuts of meat into tender eats. That's ideal for people on a tight budget, and for anyone who loves the taste of good stews and barbecue.

Pretty much impossible to burn food: Slow cookers cook food low and slow, so even if you cook something longer than you planned, changes are the food is going to be just fine. Certain ingredients, especially vegetables, can get mushy, but nothing will ever burn.

Saves energy: Turning on the oven for an hour or so eats up a lot of energy, while a slow cooker uses significantly less. That can make a big difference by the time the electrical bill comes in, and it's good for the environment.

It makes clean-up easy: Because a slow cooker is the perfect way to create one-pot meals, there isn't as much to clean up as there would be if you used a bunch of skillets, pots, and baking dishes. Less cleaning up also saves on water.

Meals are easy to transport: The slow cooker has been a staple of parties for decades, thanks to how easy the cooker is to transport. Companies have even created lids with this purpose in mind, so you can stick the slow cooker in the back of a car and don't have to worry about the lid popping off.

Disadvantages

Slow cooking isn't perfect, so it's good to be aware of some of the disadvantages. There aren't many, and the more you cook with it, the more you can adjust it to be better.

Slow cookers aren't great for fish: Slow cookers have a reputation for not cooking fish well, with the exceptions of chowders or stews. However, using the slow cooker as a kind of steamer, with the fish in a packet of foil, is a very effective way to solve this problem. You'll find recipes in the "Seafood" section that follow this recommendation.

Accumulated vapor can water down flavor: Since the water vapor that the cooker generates does not escape, it can dilute the flavors of whatever you're cooking. Using lots of spices and seasoning after the cooker is done is a great way to retain and add flavor.

__The longer you cook something, the more nutrients are lost__: Because slow cooking takes so long, that means more nutrients are lost. That can be a problem when you're cooking vegetables and other ingredients specifically for their health value. Luckily, the nutrients don't just disappear - they go into the water vapor that stays in the cooker and mixes with the meal. Sauces that are cooked with vegetables and meat in the slow cooker will retain those nutrients. That's another reason why you want to be sure to not add too much liquid, because any liquid you don't consume represents lost vitamins and minerals.

Chapter 4: Slow Cooking and a Whole Food Diet

Diet fads come and go, but there's one healthy lifestyle that has been existing in one form or another for a long time. It's the "whole food" way of life, and it's made a lot easier by a slow cooker. What exactly are whole foods? These are foods that haven't been altered or stripped with the use of artificial ingredients or add-ins, and are as close to their source as possible. This means organic fruit and veggies, whole grains, wild-caught fish, grass-fed meats, and so on.

Whole foods are the best and most natural way to improve your health and stay strong against disease. These are the reasons why everyone should eat more whole foods:

<u>*More phytonutrients*</u> - These little guys include antioxidants like lycopene (found in tomatoes) and others that are found in plants. They can help break down bad fat and cholesterol, and perform other important functions in the human body that keep us healthy. Over the last decade, food scientists have discovered hundreds of phytonutrients in the "whole," original version of plants.

**More vitamins** - People aren't eating enough vitamins, like vitamin C, vitamin A, Fiber, and more. Some think that gulping down supplements is the way to go, but the single best way to get more vitamins is to get them from their sources. You can get all you need from whole foods, especially plants.

**Less bad fat, more good fat** - "Fat" is seen as a bad word, but only certain fats like trans and saturated fats are actually harmful. Eating more whole foods like fish and vegetables allows you to consume the healthy fats like omega-3 and monounsaturated fat, while cutting out processed foods reduces your intake of bad fat.

**More fiber** - Fiber helps with so many functions, like weight loss and reduced risk of heart disease. Processed foods have most of the fiber stripped out, while whole foods are rich in them. Eating more fiber will help you feel full faster after eating less, which helps keep off the excess pounds.

**Less junk** - Processed food is packed with unnecessary, harmful junk like sodium and sugar. It seems like just about everything has an absurd amount of sugar in it, so by switching to whole foods, you're only getting what nature intended. That means more energy, less illness, and a better life.

How does slow cooking fit into whole foods?

So, you know a whole food-based diet is good for you, but what does that have to do with a slow cooker? A slow cooker is a fantastic way to embrace whole foods and a healthier lifestyle, without drastically changing your routines. Here are some key reasons:

Slow cookers make healthy cooking easier - One of the main reasons why people don't eat healthy is because it takes a lot of time and energy. Grabbing something frozen and processed, or running through a drive-thru is preferable over chopping and cooking. A slow cooker basically does all the cooking work for you, so eating healthy meals is no longer a huge chore.

Eating home-cooked meals reduces the number of processed meals - Even if you weren't embracing a whole food diet, cooking at home equals less processed meals. Once you add in the whole food element and start making smarter choices when it comes to brands and ingredients, your intake of processed and artificial food plummets.

Slow cooking retains more nutrients than some other cooking methods - Frying or boiling food causes a lot of nutrients to get lost. With slow cooking, nutrients enter the liquid part of the meal, which you can consume as sauce, thereby enjoying more of the good stuff that makes you healthy. Slow cooking also destroys less nutrients because of the low temperature.

Slow cooking keeps healthy eating interesting - Another misconception about healthy eating is that it's boring. However, there are so many recipes for slow cookers in books and online, many of which are specifically-tailored for whole foods. You don't have to eat the same five meals all the time and become so burned out that you give up on your health. Meal diversity is key to being consistent with healthy eating, and the slow cooker is up to the task.

Chapter 5: Whole-Food Pantry Staples

Always having these staples on hand ensures that every meal and snack is whole-food approved. Whenever you can, choose organic brands, and always read ingredient labels to make sure there's no artificial ingredients sneakily added in. Looking at ingredient labels also helps you pick the brands with the least amount of sugar possible. When you're building your pantry, you want to consider proteins, vegetables, stocks, and flavorings that allow you to make satisfying and nutrient-dense breakfasts, lunches, dinners, and snacks.

What you should have in your freezer:

- ✓ Lean grass-fed ground beef
- ✓ Organic ground chicken
- ✓ Frozen fish (tilapia, salmon)
- ✓ Frozen vegetables (no sauces added)
- ✓ Frozen berries (no sugar added)

What you should have in your fridge:

- ✓ Organic eggs

- ✓ Organic vegetable broth
- ✓ Organic meat stock (chicken, beef)
- ✓ Organic whole milk
- ✓ Unsweetened organic plain almond milk
- ✓ Grass-fed butter
- ✓ Unsweetened plain Greek yogurt
- ✓ Fresh lemon/lime juice

What you should have in your grain cupboard:

- ✓ Whole-wheat flour
- ✓ Whole-grain bread
- ✓ Corn tortillas
- ✓ Brown rice
- ✓ Steel-cut oats
- ✓ Rolled oats
- ✓ Whole-wheat/whole-grain pasta

What you should have in your canned goods cupboard:

- ✓ Canned black/kidney beans (no salt added)
- ✓ Dried beans
- ✓ Raw nuts (almonds, walnuts)
- ✓ Raw seeds (sunflower, pumpkin)
- ✓ All-natural, no added salt nut butter
- ✓ Canned organic tomatoes
- ✓ Organic full-fat coconut milk
- ✓ Unsweetened dried fruit

What you should have in your spices/oils cupboard:

- ✓ High-quality balsamic vinegar
- ✓ High-quality olive oil
- ✓ Organic coconut oil
- ✓ Organic soy sauce
- ✓ Organic apple cider vinegar

- ✓ Salt
- ✓ Black pepper
- ✓ Herbs + spices (cinnamon, curry powder, onion powder, garlic powder, Italian seasoning, etc.)

A word on sweeteners

On a whole-food diet, it's best to avoid sweeteners when possible. You can sweeten your food using fruit, spices, and even vegetables. Apples, bananas, prunes, and dates are all very sweet, even in their unrefined, whole state. However, sometimes you do need an actual sugar in a recipe, so stick to the following:

- Organic coconut sugar
- Organic honey
- Pure maple syrup

Another way to reduce the amount of sugar in your diet is to just use less sugar, when it's used in savory recipes or glazes. If it's baking, it's best to stick to the true measurements since it will affect the finished product.

What can you drink?

Water is the most important beverage on a whole food diet. However, you can also drink tea, milk, coffee, and 100% fruit juices. Whether or not alcohol is allowed depends on how strict you want to be, though I say it's okay in moderation, and if it doesn't include really-sugary wine coolers and flavored beers. Juice should also be a special treat, because it is so full of sugar. If you want juice, just eat the fruit it comes from.

What not to eat and drink

What about the forbidden foods? Here's what you need to avoid on a whole-food diet:

- ☒ **<u>Refined grains</u>** - white flour, white rice, sugary cereal, white bread, pastries
- ☒ **<u>Anything from a box</u>** - Look at the ingredient list, and you'll probably see a bunch of artificial stuff pretty quickly.
- ☒ **<u>Refined sugars</u>** - cane juice, corn syrup, white sugar, ice cream, candy, candy bars, frozen yogurt
- ☒ **<u>Artificial sweeteners</u>** - Splenda, Equal, etc.
- ☒ **<u>Fast food</u>** - McDonald's, Wendy's, Burger King
- ☒ **<u>Anything with carrageenan</u>** - Watch out for this ingredient in some almond
- ☒ **<u>Milks.</u>**
- ☒ **<u>Diet foods (low-fat, low-carb)</u>** - Yogurts, diet drinks, butter substitutes
- ☒ **<u>Factory-farmed meats</u>** - pork and fish are especially processed, so be careful about these in particular
- ☒ **<u>Coffee-shop coffee drinks-</u>** Unless you know exactly what a shop (Starbucks, Dutch Bros, Caribou, etc.) is putting in their drinks and it's whole-food friendly, it's best to make your own coffee mochas and lattes. However, if you drink black, feel free to order plain black coffee.

Chapter 6: A Month of Slow Cooker Whole Foods

When you change your lifestyle and start eating slow-cooked whole foods, your body begins to change for the better. A month or 30 days is a good benchmark for change after a major diet change, but a lot of benefits from eating whole foods might start appearing even after a few weeks! Here are just a few of the benefits you'll begin enjoying:

More energy

When you eat whole foods instead of processed, the body doesn't have to work as hard to digest what you put in it. On a whole foods diet, you're also eating more vegetables than probably before, and veggies provide slow-burning carbs that are essential to energy. With a plant-plentiful diet, you'll feel more energetic and productive.

Improved digestion

When it comes to digestion, fiber is where it's at. Processed foods have been stripped of fiber, while whole foods like whole grains and veggies are full of both insoluble and soluble fibers. While a lot of fiber after very little fiber can be a shock to your system, more gradually increasingly-fibrous foods like beans helps regulate your digestive system.

Better blood sugar

When you're eating a lot of processed foods and refined sugar, your blood sugar is all over the place. That leads to intense cravings, mood swings, and "crashes" that can turn any day into a bad one. When you eat more vegetables and fiber, your blood sugar levels become more stable, which is key to preventing and managing diabetes.

Less hunger and cravings

Processed food is full of calories, but leaves you feeling hungry again very quickly. Your body also goes through cravings because it misses certain nutrients. When you eat healthier foods, those cravings are satisfied, and you feel satisfied more easily thanks to fiber. You'll also experience less sugar cravings when you reduce the amount of sugar in your diet. By giving up ice cream, candy, and other refined sugars, you'll find you crave them less as time goes on. You'll also find that whole foods like fruit taste much sweeter and delicious!

Possible weight loss

The last benefit you might see after a month of slow-cooked whole foods is weight loss, if you've been carrying excess weight. Processed foods are full of ingredients that make weight loss difficult, so without those in your life, the pounds might begin to fall off.

Tips for continued success

A whole-food lifestyle isn't a "diet" in the sense that it only lasts until you meet certain goals. Ideally, it should be something you can continue for years to come, so you can reap countless benefits and just be happier. Here are some tips that can help you stay consistent:

#1: Only eat when you're hungry

This is a rule that most people aren't very good at. People tend to eat when

they're tired or bored or angry, so really learn how to listen to your body and what it needs. Staying hydrated can help a lot, as what we think are hunger pangs are very often our bodies just asking for water.

#2: Try keeping to a meal schedule

Another reason why it can be hard to know when we're hungry or not is because we eat at random times every day. Sticking to a schedule can help remind us when we actually need food, and it can help with snacking too much and overeating. Studies have shown that eating at consistent times helps keep blood sugar level stable, and helps keep digestion working the way it should.

#3: Slow down and savor

Taking the time to slow down and savor your meal is a good way to prevent overeating. It gives your body time to process what it's consumed, and let your brain know that you're full. Eating more slowly also lets you really enjoy the awesome meals you're making in your slow cooker.

#4: Make meal plans

People who plan their meals on a weekly basis save grocery money, and they are less likely to run out and get fast food because they can't think of what to cook. When you make a plan, you know exactly what you need to get at the store, and you can time your prep and anything else you need to do before letting the slow cooker do its thing.

#5: Treat yourself, but in smart ways

It's important to reward yourself when you're doing well, but you want to do it in a smart way. That means not treating yourself with forbidden food, but instead going with whole-food healthy options like one of the desserts in this cookbook (hello, cocoa-roasted almonds!) or a special homemade latte. Ideally, don't even reward yourself with food! Buy a new book, go into work a few hours late to sleep in, or go do something fun that you haven't done in a while. There are countless ways to celebrate a victory that don't involve feeling guilty afterwards.

Chapter 7 - Breakfast

One of the best things about the slow cooker is that you can make your breakfasts the night before. The cooker does its magic safely all through the night, so you wake up to the delicious aromas of bacon, eggs, or toasty oats. This section includes plenty of variations on breakfast casseroles and quiches, as well as oats, granola, and even yogurt!

Breakfast Casserole 24

Cauliflower-Sausage Breakfast Casserole 25

Spinach + Feta Quiche 27

Veggie Omelet... 28

Stuffed Peppers 30

Ham + Spinach Frittata 31

Breakfast Quinoa with Apple and Dates 33

Blueberry + Peach Steel-Cut Oats....................................... 34

Slow Cooker Granola..35

Slow Cooker Yogurt 37

CHAPTER 7 : BREAKFAST

Breakfast Casserole

Serves: 6
Time: 7 hours, 25 minutes (5 minutes prep time, 7 hours cook time, 20 minutes cool time)

There's nothing like waking up to a delicious breakfast to get your day going. This casserole can cook overnight (6-7 hours) on low. It has hash browns, eggs, ham, spinach, and bell peppers, so it's tasty and full of nutrients to fuel your day.

Ingredients:

4 eggs
2 ½ cups thawed frozen hash browns
1 ½ cups bell pepper strips
1 ½ cups cooked ham
1 cup milk
1 diced yellow onion
⅔ cup fresh spinach
½ teaspoon salt
½ teaspoon black pepper

Directions:

1. Layer the hash browns, peppers, spinach, onion, and ham in your slow cooker.
2. In a bowl, mix eggs, milk, salt, and black pepper.
3. Pour into the cooker and put on the lid.
4. Cook on low for 6-7 hours.
5. Uncover the lid and cool for 20 minutes before serving!

Nutritional Info (⅙ recipe per serving):
Total calories: 180
Protein: 15
Carbs: 13
Fat: 9
Fiber: 2

Cauliflower-Sausage Breakfast Casserole

Serves: 8-12

Time: 5-7 hours, 7 minutes (7 minutes prep time, 5-7 hours cook time)

If you're looking for a lower-carb casserole that doesn't have potatoes, use cauliflower instead. You're going to "rice" the cauliflower by pulsing it into fine grains using a food processor, and then layer on cooked sausage and cheese. This is a good breakfast recipe for holidays, when you have a lot of relatives staying over.

Ingredients:

12 eggs
Two (5-ounce) packages of cooked sausage
1 shredded (otherwise known as "riced") head of cauliflower
2 cups shredded cheddar cheese
½ cup milk
½ teaspoon dry mustard
Salt and black pepper to taste

Directions:

1. Prepare the inside of a slow cooker with a coconut-oil based cooking spray.
2. In a bowl, beat milk, eggs, salt, dry mustard, and black pepper.
3. Pour ⅓ of the riced cauliflower in your slow cooker in a single layer, and then season with salt and pepper.
4. Add ⅓ of the sausage, and then ⅓ of the cheddar cheese.
5. Repeat this layering twice, till all the cauliflower, sausage, and cheese has been used.
6. Pour over the egg mixture.
7. Cook for 5-7 hours on low.

Nutritional Info (⅛ recipe per serving):
Total calories: 371
Protein: 26
Carbs: 10
Fat: 26
Fiber: 1.5

Spinach + Feta Quiche

Serves: 5

Time: 4 hours, 5 minutes (5 minutes prep time, 4 hours cook time)

Spinach and feta cheese are a classic, sophisticated combination, but you don't need to have a lot of chef skills to make them taste delicious. You can use frozen spinach; just remember to squeeze out the water before putting it in the slow cooker. The quiche only takes 4 hours on low.

Ingredients:

4 eggs
2 cups milk
10-ounces frozen + thawed chopped spinach
4-ounces feta cheese
Dash of salt

Directions:

1. Squeeze the spinach well to get as much water out as you can.
2. Grease your slow cooker with a coconut-oil based spray.
3. In a bowl, beat the eggs.
4. Mix in the rest of the ingredients and pour into the cooker.
5. Cook on low for 4 hours.
6. Serve!

Nutritional Info (¼ recipe per serving):
Total calories: 205
Protein: 19
Carbs: 14
Fat: 13
Fiber: 1.6

CHAPTER 7 : BREAKFAST

Veggie Omelet

Serves: 4
Time: 2 hours, 5 minutes (5 minutes prep time, 2 hours cook time)

Did you know you can make omelets in your slow cooker? They only take about 2 hours on the high-heat setting. This omelet is packed with vegetables like broccoli and red bell peppers, as well as garlic and cheese. It's a healthy, protein-packed breakfast.

Ingredients:

6 eggs
1 cup broccoli florets
1 sliced red bell pepper
½ cup milk
1 chopped onion
1 chopped tomato
1 minced garlic clove
Sprinkle of sharp cheddar cheese
Salt and pepper to taste

Directions:

1. Prepare your slow cooker with a coconut-oil based cooking spray.
2. In a bowl, mix your eggs, milk, salt, and pepper.
3. Mix in the broccoli, onions, garlic, and peppers.
4. Pour into the slow cooker.
5. Cook on high for 2 hours.
6. Sprinkle in cheese.
7. When melted, cut into pieces and serve with chopped tomatoes.

Nutritional Info (¼ recipe per serving):
Total calories: 196
Protein: 16
Carbs: 14
Fat: 10
Fiber: 1.7

CHAPTER 7 : BREAKFAST

Stuffed Peppers

Serves: 4
Time: 3-4 hours, 5 minutes (5 minutes prep time, 3-4 hours cook time)

I love bell peppers because they're basically vegetable bowls ready to be stuffed with awesome ingredients like eggs and bacon. This recipe cooks four bell peppers, any color you want, with a mixture of raw eggs, cooked bacon, and green onions for 3-4 hours on low. When they're done, sprinkle on a little cheese and enjoy!

Ingredients:

4 halved and seeded bell peppers
5 eggs
4 crumbled pieces of cooked bacon
1 cup cheddar cheese
½ cup milk
2 tablespoons chopped green onion
Salt and pepper to taste

Directions:

1. Mix eggs in a bowl.
2. Add in milk, bacon, green onion, salt, and pepper.
3. Prepare your slow cooker with a crockpot liner and put in the peppers.
4. Fill peppers evenly with your egg mixture.
5. Cook on low for 3-4 hours.
6. Sprinkle with cheese before serving.

Nutritional Info (¼ recipe per serving):
Total calories: 282
Protein: 20
Carbs: 11
Fat: 19
Fiber: 2.5

Ham + Spinach Frittata

Serves: 4
Time: 1.5-2 hours, 6 minutes (6 minutes prep time, 1 ½ - 2 hours cook time)

Frittatas are crustless quiches, and they're great for getting in lots of vegetables and meat. This recipe adds ham, mushrooms, and baby spinach for a nutrient and protein-packed meal. It also uses Greek yogurt instead of milk to ensure the eggs are creamy and delicious. Season with plenty of onion powder, thyme, salt, black pepper, and garlic powder.

Ingredients:

6 eggs
1 cup baby spinach
1 cup diced cooked ham
1 cup shredded cheddar cheese
½ cup Greek yogurt
⅓ cup diced button mushrooms
¼ cup milk
½ teaspoon onion powder
½ teaspoon salt
½ teaspoon thyme
½ teaspoon black pepper
½ teaspoon garlic powder

Directions:

1. Mix eggs, milk, yogurt, and spices in a bowl.
2. Add spinach, cheese, ham, and mushrooms.
3. Grease your slow cooker with a coconut-oil based cooking spray and pour in the egg mixture.
4. Cook on high for 1.5-2 hours.
5. Serve hot!

Nutritional Info (¼ recipe per serving):
Total calories: 312
Protein: 30
Carbs: 5
Fat: 19
Fiber: 1

Breakfast Quinoa with Apple and Dates

Serves: 4
Time: 2-8 hours

Quinoa is often overlooked as a breakfast food, but it's natural nuttiness and high nutrients make it a great choice. In this recipe, quinoa is cooked with almond milk, an apple, and dates. No additional sugar is needed; just season with a bit of cinnamon, vanilla, and salt!

Ingredients:

3 cups almond milk
1 cup quinoa
1 peeled and diced apple
4 chopped Medjool dates
2 teaspoons cinnamon
1 teaspoon pure vanilla extract
¼ teaspoon salt

Directions:

1. Put all the ingredients in your slow cooker.
2. Cook on high for 2 hours, or overnight on low for 8 hours.
3. Serve!

Nutritional Info (¼ recipe per serving):
Total calories: 291
Protein: 7
Carbs: 54
Fat: 5
Fiber: 3.25

CHAPTER 7 : BREAKFAST

Blueberry + Peach Steel-Cut Oats

Serves: 6
Time: 8 hours

Steel-cut oats are one of my favorite hearty breakfasts, especially when the morning is chilly and gloomy. You're going to mix oats and almond milk with frozen peaches and blueberries and cook on low for 8 hours, so it's a great recipe to make the night before. Vanilla and cinnamon add a lovely sweet-spiciness.

Ingredients:

4 cups almond milk
4 cups water
3 cups steel-cut oats
1 pound frozen peaches
2 cups frozen blueberries
1 tablespoon pure vanilla extract
2 teaspoons cinnamon

Directions:

1. Grease your slow cooker with a coconut oil-based cooking spray.
2. Mix everything in your slow cooker and close the lid.
3. Cook on low for 8 hours.
4. Serve!

Nutritional Info (⅙ recipe per serving):
Total calories: 393
Protein: 9
Carbs: 69
Fat: 7
Fiber: 10

Slow Cooker Granola

Makes: 5 cups
Time: 2 hours, 6 minutes (6 minutes prep time, 2 hours cook time)

Granola is one of those "health" foods that's often anything but healthy. Store-bought versions are packed with sugar. When you make your own, you can control the sweetness level. This recipe uses honey, raisins, and vanilla to sweeten, while including protein-laden chunky peanut butter and almonds. Remember to stir the granola every half hour while it cooks for 2 hours on high, so everything toasts evenly.

Ingredients:

5 cups old-fashioned rolled oats
⅔ cup honey
½ cup raisins
½ cup organic chunky peanut butter
⅓ cup melted coconut oil
5 tablespoons slivered almonds
1 tablespoon pure vanilla extract
2 teaspoons cinnamon
¼ teaspoon salt

Directions:

1. Grease your slow cooker with a coconut-oil based spray.
2. Add oats, slivered almonds, and salt.
3. In a bowl, mix honey, coconut oil, cinnamon, vanilla, and peanut butter.
4. Microwave for a minute, stir, and then microwave for 30 seconds at a time until everything is smooth and combined.
5. Pour over the oats in your cooker and stir, so the oats are completely coated.
6. Put the lid on the cooker; you want it slightly askew, to vent the cooker. The slow cooker will still work.

7. Cook for 2 hours on high, pausing to stir the granola every 30 minutes.
8. Add raisins and spread across a baking sheet to cool.
9. Store in an airtight container.

Nutritional Info (½ cup per serving):
Total calories: 421
Protein: 11
Carbs: 54
Fat: 19
Fiber: 5.6

Slow Cooker Yogurt

Serves: 6

Time: 4-6 hours, 30 minutes (30 minutes prep time, 4-6 hours wait time)

Making yogurt is way easier than you probably ever imagined! All you need is half a gallon of organic whole milk and ½ cup plain yogurt, which will act as your yogurt "starter." You also need a cooking thermometer, because temperature is very important in this recipe. This recipe makes six servings of plain yogurt, making it a blank canvas for add-ins like fruit. If you want your yogurt as healthy as possible, use as little sweeteners as possible, and stick to berries.

Ingredients:

½ gallon organic whole milk
½ cup plain yogurt

Directions:

1. Pour milk into your slow cooker.
2. Tie a cooking thermometer to your cooker, so it's in the milk, but won't fall in.
3. Hit "boil" and stir till the milk reaches 200-degrees F.
4. Turn off the cooker.
5. Ladle out some milk and pour into a bowl.
6. Mix in the yogurt till smooth.
7. Once the milk in the cooker has descended to 112 degrees, pour in the yogurt/milk mixture.
8. Whisk until smooth.
9. Put the lid on the cooker and wait 4 hours. For a thicker yogurt, wait 6 hours.
10. When time is up, move your yogurt into a jar and stick in the fridge. Wait overnight before eating.

Nutritional Info (½ cup per serving):
Total calories: 213
Protein: 11
Carbs: 17
Fat: 11
Fiber: 0

Chapter 8 - Poultry

Chicken and turkey are two of the most affordable and versatile proteins you can buy. It's easy to make really simple, weekday meals, and also fancier ones for holidays or parties. This section has poultry recipes inspired by Mexican, Asian, and Mediterranean cultures, so even if you had chicken every day of the week, you wouldn't get sick of it thanks to the diversity of flavors and spices.

Chicken with Tomatoes and Peppers *40*
Easy Chicken Curry *42*
Fiesta Chicken with Beans *44*
Chicken Stew *45*
Sweet 'n Sour Chicken *46*
Garlic Rosemary Chicken + Potatoes *48*
Italian Sausage, Turkey, and Potatoes *49*
Chicken with Fire-Roasted Tomatoes *50*
Chicken Chili *51*
Parmesan Garlic Chicken with Orzo and Vegetables *52*
Chipotle Turkey Chili with Apples *54*
Mediterranean-Spiced Roast Turkey *56*

Chicken with Tomatoes and Peppers

Serves: 4
Time: 5 hours, 5 minutes (5 minutes prep time, 5 hours cook time)

This colorful meal embraces the red vegetables - red bell peppers and tomatoes. The red peppers have the most vitamin C of any of the bell peppers, and are a good source of fiber. They add a sweetness that is contrasted with the garlic, onion, and Dijon mustard. The tomatoes also add a sweet flavor, and help ensure the chicken is tender and moist.

Ingredients:

3 pounds chicken breasts
½ cup white wine
2 sliced red bell peppers
1 can diced tomatoes
1 chopped onion
4 minced garlic cloves
2 tablespoons Dijon mustard
1 teaspoon ground thyme
Salt and pepper to taste
Splash of olive oil

Directions:

1. Grease the slow cooker insides with olive oil and a paper towel.
2. Dry the chicken with a clean paper towel.
3. Rub chicken with Dijon mustard, salt, pepper, and thyme.
4. Put chicken in the cooker and pour over wine and vegetables.
5. Put the lid on the cooker and set for 5 hours on high.

Nutritional Info (¼ recipe per serving):
Total calories: 502
Protein: 70
Carbs: 11
Fat: 4
Fiber: 1.5

CHAPTER 8: POULTRY

Easy Chicken Curry

Serves: 4-6

Time: 2.5-3 hours, 5 minutes (5 minutes prep time, 2.5-3 hours cook time)

Chicken curry is a favorite of mine, because of the fantastic spices, but it might not be familiar to a lot of people. If you think all Indian food is too spicy, never fear, you can control the amount of spice by using very little curry powder, and going with a milder one. The heat in this recipe is smoothed out by full-fat coconut milk. If you want, you can serve the curry with rice, though the cubed red potatoes with the chicken thighs might be enough for you!

Ingredients:

1 ½ pounds chicken thighs
One 15-ounce can diced tomatoes
1 pound cubed red potatoes
¾ cup full-fat coconut milk
1 small diced onion
1-2 tablespoons curry powder
1 tablespoon minced ginger
½ teaspoon salt

Directions:

1. Grease your slow cooker before putting in the potatoes and chicken thighs.
2. Mix in coconut milk, tomatoes, onion, ginger, curry, and salt in a bowl.
3. Pour over the chicken and close the lid.
4. Cook for 2.5-3 hours on high.
5. Serve with rice!

Nutritional Info (¼ recipe per serving):
Total calories: 383
Protein: 37
Carbs: 27
Fat: 14
Fiber: 4.5

CHAPTER 8: POULTRY

Fiesta Chicken with Beans

Serves: 4
Time: 5-6 hours

This is one of the easiest dinners you can make. All you have to do is throw a bunch of ingredients in your slow cooker and cook for 5-6 hours. The meal is packed with corn, black beans, diced tomato, onion, and green bell pepper. For seasoning, it's just salt, pepper, chili powder, and cumin, which is a must for Mexican-inspired dishes.

Ingredients:

4 boneless chicken breasts
One 15-ounce can of drained corn
One 15-ounce can of rinsed and drained black beans
One 14-ounce can of diced tomatoes
6-ounces tomato paste
1 sliced onion
1 sliced green bell pepper
1 tablespoon cumin
1 teaspoon chili powder
Salt and pepper to taste

Directions:

1. Mix everything in the slow cooker.
2. Cook for 5-6 hours on high.
3. Serve!

Nutritional Info (¼ recipe per serving):
Total calories: 308
Protein: 30
Carbs: 28
Fat: 3
Fiber: 9.5

Chicken Stew

Serves: 4
Time: 5-6 hours

Classic and easy, this chicken stew recipe just involves tossing a bunch of ingredients in your slow cooker and cooking on high for 5-6 hours. It's a great recipe to make in the morning before you go off to work, and dinner is ready when you get back home. It's got lots of seasonings, like garlic, cumin, and chili powder, that make the stew taste even better the next day after they've had a chance to really marinate.

Ingredients:

4 boneless chicken breasts
3 cups organic chicken broth
2 cans undrained diced tomatoes
2 cups rinsed and drained yellow hominy
3 sliced carrots
3 sliced green onions
3 minced garlic cloves
1 tablespoon cumin
2 teaspoons chili powder
1 teaspoon oregano
Salt and black pepper to taste

Directions:

1. Put the chicken in your slow cooker.
2. Add everything and stir.
3. Cook on high for 5-6 hours.
4. Shred before serving!

Nutritional Info (¼ recipe per serving):

Total calories: 292
Protein: 35
Carbs: 27
Fat: 3
Fiber: 3

Sweet 'n Sour Chicken

Serves: 4
Time: 4-5 hours, 5 minutes (5 minutes prep time, 4-5 hours cook time)

A staple of American-Chinese takeout menus, this sweet and sour chicken is healthier and very easy to make. We try to avoid sugar of any kind in this book, but for this recipe, you do need just 1 tablespoon of coconut sugar. The rest of the sweetness comes from crushed pineapple and apple cider vinegar. You can make the chicken using frozen tenders, so even if you forget to thaw them, you can still make this addicting meal.

Ingredients:

2 pounds frozen chicken tenders
One 20-ounce can of crushed pineapple
¼ cup apple cider vinegar
¼ cup water
2 sliced red bell peppers
1 small sliced onion
1 crushed clove of garlic
2 tablespoons cornstarch
1 tablespoon coconut sugar
1 tablespoon organic soy sauce
½ teaspoon salt
¼ teaspoon ground ginger

Directions:

1. Put chicken, peppers, and onion in the slow cooker.
2. Drain the can of pineapple, and add the juice to the pot. You'll add pineapple later.
3. Add the rest of the ingredients on top of the chicken.
4. Cook on high for 4-5 hours.
5. Before serving, mix in pineapple and serve with brown rice!

Nutritional Info (¼ recipe per serving):
Total calories: 381
Protein: 55
Carbs: 35
Fat: 3
Fiber: 1.5

CHAPTER 8: POULTRY

Garlic Rosemary Chicken + Potatoes

Serves: 4
Time: 5-6 hours

Garlic and rosemary are two of my favorite flavor combinations. They're rustic and earthy, but also fresh. You're going to be using 10 whole garlic cloves for 3 pounds of chicken, and two sprigs of fresh rosemary. All the ingredients go in the slow cooker at once, no browning or anything needed beforehand, and are cooked in white wine for 5-6 hours.

Ingredients:

3 pounds boneless chicken breasts
10 peeled, whole garlic cloves
7 chopped medium-sized red potatoes
2 sprigs fresh rosemary
1 sliced onion
½ cup white wine
Salt and pepper to taste

Directions:

1. Add everything to the slow cooker, with wine poured on top.
2. Cook on high for 5-6 hours.
3. Serve!

Nutritional Info (¼ recipe per serving):
Total calories: 587
Protein: 72
Carbs: 33
Fat: 4
Fiber: 3

Italian Sausage, Turkey, and Potatoes

Serves: 6
Time: 5-6 hours

Meat lovers, rejoice! This recipe has two kinds of meat: turkey legs and turkey sausage. They're accompanied by white potatoes, garlic, and diced tomatoes seasoned with fennel and red pepper. It's a great meal for cold evenings after you've been on your feet all day.

Ingredients:

2 pounds turkey legs
1 ¼ pounds sweet Italian turkey sausage
One 15-ounce can of diced tomatoes (with red pepper and fennel)
6 chopped white potatoes
4 whole garlic cloves
1 sliced onion
Salt and pepper to taste

Directions:

1. Put everything in the slow cooker, meat-first.
2. Cook on high for 5-6 hours.
3. Serve!

Nutritional Info (⅙ recipe per serving):
Total calories: 415
Protein: 34
Carbs: 34
Fat: 15
Fiber: 8.8

CHAPTER 8: POULTRY

Chicken with Fire-Roasted Tomatoes

Serves: 4
Time: 4 hours

It doesn't get simpler than this: bone-in chicken breasts and fire-roasted tomatoes. These two main ingredients are joined by onion, garlic, salt, and chili powder. That's all you need for a flavorful, healthy meal for four.

Ingredients:

3 large bone-in chicken breasts
One 15-ounce can of fire-roasted tomatoes
1 chopped onion
3 chopped garlic cloves
Salt to taste
Chili powder to taste

Directions:

1. Put chicken in the slow cooker.
2. Add everything on top and close the lid.
3. Cook on high for 4 hours.
4. Serve hot!

Nutritional Info (¼ recipe per serving):
Total calories: 177
Protein: 27
Carbs: 8
Fat: 8
Fiber: 1.7

Chicken Chili

Serves: 4
Time: 5 hours

This chili is a great way to use up leftover chicken. You'll need about 3 cups' worth. For vegetables, I love zucchinis, and we're using two kinds of beans. For the salsa, be sure to go with an organic brand that isn't full of processed ingredients. You can also use your own if you have some on hand. Cook everything for 5 hours, season, and enjoy!

Ingredients:

3 cups cooked shredded chicken breasts
5 cups chicken broth
3 chopped zucchinis
2 cups chunky salsa (your favorite)
2 cups pinto beans
2 cups black beans
One 8-ounce can of tomato sauce
1 cup frozen corn
Salt and pepper to taste

Directions:

1. Mix everything in the slow cooker.
2. Cook on high for 5 hours.
3. Season to taste with salt and pepper.
4. Serve!

Nutritional Info (¼ recipe per serving):
Total calories: 479
Protein: 37
Carbs: 63
Fat: 7
Fiber: 15.7

Parmesan Garlic Chicken with Orzo and Vegetables

Serves: 6
Time: 6 hours (1 hour marinade time, 5 hours cook time)

Orzo is a pasta, though it looks like a rice, and is an Italian classic. Go with whole-wheat. The vegetables can be anything you like or whatever is in season. To ensure great flavor, marinate the chicken breasts in salt, pepper, Italian seasoning, olive oil, garlic, and a little wine. Overnight is ideal, but one hour does the trick, too. The orzo itself does not cook in the slow cooker, that's where the chicken goes. Just follow the directions on the orzo box. The fresh vegetables get added at the very end, since they don't need to cook. A sprinkle of Parmesan cheese brings everything together, and dinner's ready!

Ingredients:

4 boneless, skinless chicken breasts
1 cup dry whole-wheat orzo
¾ cup mixed fresh vegetables (zucchinis, tomatoes, carrot, onion, etc.)
¼ cup + 2 tablespoons grated Parmesan cheese
6 tablespoons white wine
4 tablespoons olive oil
4 minced garlic cloves
1 tablespoon Italian seasoning
Salt to taste

Directions:

1. Season chicken with salt, pepper, and Italian seasoning.
2. In a bag, mix 3 tablespoons of olive oil, garlic, and 3 tablespoons of wine.
3. Add chicken and marinate for at least one hour.
4. When ready, pour 3 tablespoons of wine in your cooker

and add chicken.
5. Cook on high for 5 hours.
6. When there's about 10 minutes left on the slow cooker, cook orzo as directed on the box.
7. Mix cooked orzo with olive oil, parmesan, and salt.
8. Cut chicken and toss with orzo and vegetables.
9. Sprinkle on some more parmesan cheese before serving!

Nutritional Info (⅙ recipe per serving):
Total calories: 299
Protein: 19
Carbs: 22
Fat: 12
Fiber: 2

CHAPTER 8: POULTRY

Chipotle Turkey Chili with Apples

Serves: 4-6
Time: 4-6 hours, 5 minutes (5 minutes prep time, 4-6 hours cook time)

Turkey chili is a tasty and healthier version of beef chili, and when you add spicy ingredients like chipotle peppers, and sweeter ones like apples and cider, you get an explosion of flavor that only gets better over time. There's no browning necessary for this recipe; simply add your ingredients to cook and mix them up, and cook on high for 4-6 hours.

Ingredients:

2 pounds ground turkey
One 15-ounce can of tomato sauce
One 8-ounce container of organic chicken broth
2 cored and chopped apples
1 chopped yellow onion
1 cup apple cider
1-2 chopped chipotle peppers (in adobo sauce)
2 minced garlic cloves
Juice from one lime
1 bay leaf
2 teaspoons cumin
1 teaspoon sea salt

Directions:

1. Put the meat, tomato sauce, chicken broth, cider, onion, garlic, peppers, cumin, salt, and bay leaf in the slow cooker.
2. Break up the turkey a bit with a spatula and mix in the sauce.
3. Cook on high for 4-6 hours.
4. Add lime juice and season with more salt if necessary.
5. Serve!

Nutritional Info (¼ recipe per serving):
Total calories: 594
Protein: 68
Carbs: 27
Fat: 25
Fiber: 2

CHAPTER 8: POULTRY

Mediterranean-Spiced Roast Turkey

Serves: 8
Time: 5 hours, 30 minutes

Looking for something unique to serve at Thanksgiving? Try this roast turkey that's spiced with flavors straight from the Greek islands. There's kalamata olives, sun-dried tomatoes, and Greek seasoning, which includes basil, oregano, dill, and more. The recipe also makes its own gravy thanks to a little flour and broth.

Ingredients:

4 pounds boneless turkey breasts
2 cups chopped onion
½ cup chicken stock
½ cup pitted kalamata olives
½ cup sun-dried tomatoes
3 tablespoons flour
2 tablespoons lemon juice
1 ½ teaspoons minced garlic
1 teaspoon Greek seasoning mix
Salt and pepper to taste

Directions:

1. Mix ¼ cup chicken broth with all the ingredients (except flour) in the slow cooker.
2. Cook on high for 5 hours.
3. Mix ¼ cup of broth and flour in a bowl, until smooth.
4. Pour into slow cooker.
5. Cook on low for another 30 minutes.
6. Slice turkey and serve!

Nutritional Info (⅛ recipe per serving):
Total calories: 317
Protein: 48
Carbs: 13
Fat: 8
Fiber: 1

Chapter 9 - Beef

Americans love red meat, and to get the most nutritional value, you should always go with grass-fed beef. It can be a bit pricier, but it's well worth it in every way. This section is full of recipes you can make every day of the week, including taco meat brimming with spices, spicy Sloppy Joe's, and stew made with hoisin-marinated beef.

Spice-City Beef Taco Meat 58

10-Ingredient Beef Bourguignon 60

Italian Chuck Roast with Bell Peppers and Mushrooms 62

Steak Fajitas with Fixin's 64

Spicy Sloppy Joe's 66

Ginger Beef 68

Beef + Potato Au Gratin 70

Cinnamon-Kissed Pot Roast 72

Hoisin Beef Stew 74

Bean + Beef Chili 76

Orange-Spiced Corned Beef 77

Spice-City Beef Taco Meat

Serves: 4
Time: 4 hours

This recipe is called "spice city" because of all the spices in the ingredient list. They've all been chosen to add their own twist on the beef, and they all compliment each other beautifully. The spices are found in most kitchens and include cumin, garlic powder, paprika, and crushed red pepper. You can add more of the red pepper if you like a spicier taco. On the low setting, the meat only takes 4 hours.

Ingredients:

2 pounds grass-fed ground beef
3 tablespoons tomato paste
1 tablespoon chili powder
1 teaspoon sea salt
1 teaspoon cumin
½ teaspoon dried oregano
½ teaspoon garlic powder
½ teaspoon onion powder
¼ teaspoon crushed red pepper
¼ teaspoon paprika

Directions:

1. Mix all the spices together in a bowl.
2. Add beef, tomato paste, and spices into the slow cooker and mix well.
3. Cook on low for 4 hours.
4. When time is up, make sure the meat is all broken apart before serving!

Nutritional Info (¼ recipe per serving):
Total calories: 459
Protein: 45
Carbs: 4
Fat: 29
Fiber: 0

CHAPTER 9: BEEF

10-Ingredient Beef Bourguignon

Serves: 4
Time: 6-8 hours, 20 minutes (20 minutes prep time, 6-8 hours cook time)

Beef bourguignon is essentially a rich beef stew, and it's a perfect meal to start in the morning before you leave for the day, and it's ready when you come back. There's only ten ingredients, and they include lots of aromatics like celery and carrots, and rich red wine and bacon. There's a bit of prep involved, like cooking the bacon and browning the meat, so prepare accordingly.

Ingredients:

2 ½ pounds cubed grass-fed stew beef
4 pieces bacon
2 ½ cups organic beef broth
2 cups red wine
4 carrots
4 celery ribs
1 onion
1 teaspoon salt
½ teaspoon dried thyme

Directions:

1. Cook the bacon in a large skillet until crispy.
2. Crumble bacon into your slow cooker.
3. Reserve at least one tablespoon of grease in the skillet, and remove the rest.
4. Add meat to the greased skillet, and cook until brown.
5. Spoon into the slow cooker.
6. Pour wine into the skillet, scraping up any stuck-on bits, and turn to high.
7. Keeping cooking until the wine is reduced by half.
8. Pour into your slow cooker.
9. Cook veggies in any remaining grease into the skillet for

just 2-3 minutes.
10. Put in your slow cooker with the stock and seasonings, and close the lid.
11. Cook on low for 6-8 hours.
12. Serve hot!

Nutritional Info (¼ recipe per serving):
Total calories: 531
Protein: 69
Carbs: 13
Fat: 12
Fiber: 2.5

CHAPTER 9: BEEF

Italian Chuck Roast with Bell Peppers and Mushrooms

Serves: 4
Time: 7-8 hours, 5 minutes (5 minute prep time, 7-8 hours cook time)

A hearty meal for a family of four, this recipe can be cooked overnight on low, or during the day for 7-8 hours. Bell peppers and mushrooms are earthy and rustic, and packed with nutrition. The rich sauce is made from red wine vinegar, Italian seasoning, organic Worcestershire sauce, and just a tablespoon of pure maple syrup, to bring out the natural sweetness of the onion and bell peppers.

Ingredients:

2 ½ pounds grass-fed boneless beef chuck roast
10-ounces quartered white mushrooms
⅓ cup organic beef stock
1 sliced sweet onion
1 sliced and seeded green bell pepper
1 sliced and seeded red bell pepper
2 tablespoons red wine vinegar
1 tablespoon organic Worcestershire sauce
1 tablespoon pure maple syrup
1 ¼ teaspoons Italian seasoning
Salt and black pepper to taste

Directions:

1. Grease your slow cooker with a coconut-oil based cooking spray.
2. Cut your roast into four pieces.
3. Season well with salt, pepper, and Italian seasoning.
4. Put in your cooker and add mushrooms, onion, and peppers.

5. In a bowl, mix stock, vinegar, Worcestershire, and syrup.
6. Pour over the meat.
7. Cook on low overnight for 7-8 hours.
8. Serve with the cooked vegetables and cooking liquid as sauce.

Nutritional Info (¼ recipe per serving):
Total calories: 237
Protein: 21
Carbs: 12
Fat: 14
Fiber: 1.7

CHAPTER 9: BEEF

Steak Fajitas with Fixin's

Serves: 6
Time: 5-6 hours, 5 minutes (5 minutes prep time, 5-6 hours cook time)

All you need after you make this recipe is the tortillas. The slow cooker prepares both the meat and veggies in this recipe, which uses 3 ½ pounds of flank steak, four bell peppers, an onion, and spices like cumin and coriander. A chopped jalapeno brings the heat. Once the meat is cooked and shredded, you can serve everything in a tortilla, in a sandwich, or on salad.

Ingredients:

3 ½ pounds grass-fed flank steak
4 red bell peppers
1 sliced onion
1 seeded and chopped jalapeno pepper
2 minced garlic cloves
2 tablespoons coconut aminos
1 teaspoon cumin
1 teaspoon coriander
1 ½ teaspoons chili powder
Salt and pepper to taste

Directions:

1. Mix dry spices together in a bowl.
2. Rub all over the flank steak.
3. Lay down in your slow cooker, and pour coconut aminos on top.
4. Add jalapeno, bell peppers, onion, and garlic.
5. Cook on high for 5-6 hours.
6. When done, shred the meat.
7. Drain before serving in whole-wheat tortillas or on salad!

Nutritional Info (⅛ recipe per serving):
Total calories: 562
Protein: 79
Carbs: 8
Fat: 22
Fiber: 1.5

Spicy Sloppy Joe's

Serves: 6-8
Time: 4-5 hours, 7 minutes (7 minutes prep time, 4-5 hours cook time)

Packed with mushrooms, bell peppers, and carrots, this Sloppy Joe meat isn't a meal you have to feel guilty about. Choose your salsa carefully; you want one with only real food listed in the ingredients. If you want a spice on the milder side, choose your salsa accordingly. If you like the heat, you can also add more cayenne.

Ingredients:

2 pounds grass-fed lean ground beef
Two 16-ounce jars of organic salsa
3 cups sliced mushrooms
1 ½ cups red bell pepper
1 ½ cups shredded carrots
⅓ cup tomato paste
4 minced garlic cloves
½ teaspoon salt
¼ teaspoon cayenne pepper

Directions:

1. Heat a skillet and add meat to brown.
2. Drain fat before adding to a slow cooker with the rest of the ingredients.
3. Stir well.
4. Cook on high for 4-5 hours.
5. Serve!

Nutritional Info (⅙ recipe per serving):
Total calories: 414
Protein: 33
Carbs: 25
Fat: 19
Fiber: 1

CHAPTER 9: BEEF

Ginger Beef

Serves: 4
Time: 3-4 hours, 3 minutes

Ginger really brightens up the richness of beef. Fresh ginger is the best, and other ingredients like scallions, garlic, and red bell pepper add even more acid to cut through the richness of grass-fed beef roast, sweet carrots, and sugar snap peas. When you cook the beef on high, it only takes 3-4 hours.

Ingredients:

2 pounds cubed grass-fed beef roast
3 sliced carrots
1 ½ cups organic beef stock
1 cup sugar snap peas
1 cup sliced scallions
1 chopped red bell pepper
3 minced garlic cloves
2-4 tablespoons grated fresh ginger
2 tablespoons arrowroot powder
2 tablespoons coconut aminos
1 teaspoon red pepper flakes
Salt and pepper to taste

Directions:

1. Put all the ingredients except sugar snap peas in your slow cooker.
2. Cook on high for 3-4 hours.
3. When the beef is ready, put the peas in a pot with a little water and steam for 3 minutes until they turn bright green.
4. Serve meat and peas with brown rice!

Nutritional Info (¼ recipe per serving):
Total calories: 216
Protein: 17
Carbs: 13
Fat: 11
Fiber: 2.2

Beef + Potato Au Gratin

Serves: 4
Time: 4 hours, 8 minutes (8 minutes prep time, 4 hours cook time)

Beef and potatoes are truly a match made in heaven. This take on a classic combines ground beef with cheesy potato au gratin. Spices like garlic powder, paprika, and dried parsley add some kick and freshness. The gratin is prepared in layers, with browned beef on top of potatoes, followed by cheddar cheese. The meal takes about 4 hours.

Ingredients:

3 pounds peeled and sliced russet potatoes
1 pound grass-fed ground beef
2 cups cheddar cheese
½ cup organic beef stock
1 teaspoon paprika
1 teaspoon dried parsley
½ teaspoon garlic powder
Salt and pepper to taste

Directions:

1. Heat a skillet and brown the meat with a little salt and pepper.
2. In a bowl, mix ground spices.
3. Add half of the sliced potatoes to the slow cooker, and sprinkle on half the bowl of seasonings, half the beef, and half the cheese.
4. Repeat with the remaining ingredients.
5. Cook on high for 4 hours.
6. When time is up, make sure the potatoes are soft.
7. Serve and enjoy!

Nutritional Info (¼ recipe per serving):
Total calories: 743
Protein: 45
Carbs: 61
Fat: 37
Fiber: 7.8

Cinnamon-Kissed Pot Roast

Serves: 8
Time: 8-10 hours, 26 minutes (16 minutes prep time, 8-10 hours cook time, 10 minutes rest time)

This roast would be perfect for Christmas and other winter gatherings, since it makes enough to feed 8 people. If you've never had cinnamon with beef, you're in for a treat. The chuck roast is browned, and then added to a slow cooker with diced tomatoes, onion, garlic, and whole cinnamon sticks. The cinnamon becomes infused into the sauce, giving it a distinct sweet-spiciness.

Ingredients:

2 ½ pounds grass-fed beef chuck roast
One 28-ounce can of diced tomatoes
3-4 cinnamon sticks
¼ cup chopped fresh parsley
2 chopped onions
3 minced garlic cloves
2 teaspoons olive oil
Salt and pepper to taste

Directions:

1. Heat the oil in a skillet.
2. When hot, add beef to brown.
3. Season with salt and pepper.
4. When brown, move to a slow cooker.
5. Add onions to the skillet and cook in the remaining oil and fat for about 6 minutes, or until onions are soft.
6. Add garlic and cook for another few minutes.
7. Toss in the slow cooker with tomatoes and cinnamon sticks.
8. Cook overnight for 8-10 hours.
9. When ready, take out the meat and let it rest for 10 minutes before slicing against the grain.

10. Garnish with parsley.

Nutritional Info (⅛ recipe per serving):
Total calories: 530
Protein: 39
Carbs: 8
Fat: 37
Fiber: 2

Hoisin Beef Stew

Serves: 4
Time: Overnight marinade + 3 hours cook time

Hoisin is an amazing sauce from China that is both sweet and savory, thanks to flavors from miso paste, vinegar, soy sauce, and more. When you're looking for a good brand, you want one with as few ingredients as possible, like Annie's Naturals. In addition to the beef, the hoisin should marinate the onion, garlic, and carrot overnight for really rich flavors. Cooking the stew takes only 3 hours on high, so you can start marinating the beef in the morning if you like, and cook it in the evening for dinner. It should also be fine if you marinate it overnight, and then all day before cooking.

Ingredients:

1 ½ pounds grass-fed cubed stew beef
One 10-ounce bottle of organic hoisin sauce
2 chopped onions
2 chopped celery stalks
3 minced garlic cloves
1 cup baby carrots
½ cup beef stock
1-inch piece of grated ginger

Directions:

1. Mix hoisin, stock, garlic, and ginger in a bowl.
2. Pour into a plastic baggie and add beef, onions, celery, and carrots.
3. Store in the fridge overnight to marinate.
4. When ready to cook, add everything to your slow cooker and cook on high for 3 hours.
5. Serve hot!

Nutritional Info (¼ recipe per serving):
Total calories: 430
Protein: 55
Carbs: 24
Fat: 10
Fiber: 2

CHAPTER 9: BEEF

Bean + Beef Chili

Serves: 4
Time: 7-8 hours

This chili is as classic as it gets. All the ingredients, like beef, tomatoes, kidney beans, and spices, cook overnight or all day for 7-8 hours. No real prep or browning is needed. When it's done, you just shred the beef and return it to the stew with some lime juice and extra salt if necessary.

Ingredients:

1 ½ pounds cubed grass-fed stew beef
Two 14.5-ounce cans fire-roasted tomatoes
One 15-ounce can of drained and rinsed kidney beans
1 chopped onion
1 chopped red bell pepper
1 tablespoon lime juice
1-3 teaspoons salt
1 teaspoon ground cumin
1 teaspoon garlic powder
½ teaspoon mild chili powder

Directions:

1. In a slow cooker, mix onion, bell pepper, beans, tomatoes, cumin, chili powder, salt, and meat.
2. Cook overnight for 7-8 hours.
3. Take out the beef and shred.
4. Add lime juice and more salt if necessary.
5. Enjoy!

Nutritional Info (¼ recipe per serving):

Total calories: 402
Protein: 49
Carbs: 28
Fat: 6
Fiber: 9.5

Orange-Spiced Corned Beef

Serves: 6
Time: 8-10 hours, 5 minutes (5 minutes prep time, 8-10 hours cook time)

This sweet and salty entree would be terrific with mashed cauliflower or as is with the sauce on top. The tapioca helps thicken the sauce, which is packed with dried fruit. Be sure to get the kind that doesn't have any added sugar. Corned beef is salt-cured meat, so you don't need to add salt to this recipe.

Ingredients:

3 pounds corned beef brisket
7-ounces mixed dried fruit
½ cup dried cranberries
½ cup water
½ cup no-sugar added orange juice
2 tablespoons quick-cooking tapioca
1 tablespoon pure maple syrup
¼ teaspoon ground cinnamon
⅛ teaspoon ground nutmeg

Directions:

1. Put meat in your slow cooker.
2. Add dried fruit, cranberries, and tapioca to the meat.
3. In a bowl, mix water, orange juice, maple syrup, cinnamon, and nutmeg.
4. Pour into the cooker.
5. Cook for 8-10 hours.
6. When time is up, take out the meat and let it rest for 5 minutes or so.
7. Slice meat against the grain.
8. Serve with fruit mixture.

Nutritional Info (⅙ recipe per serving):
Total calories: 617
Protein: 35
Carbs: 38
Fat: 36
Fiber: 2

Chapter 10 - Pork

Pork may be known as the "other white meat," but these recipes will make you want to feature pork on your table more often. The slow cooker does wonders with pork, which has a tendency to be overcooked and dried out, and you'll be enjoying dishes like pork loin glazed in balsamic vinegar, spicy pork ribs and tacos, and a honey-mustard ham that would be perfect for the holidays.

Apple Cider Pork Roast 80

Pork Carnitas 82

Balsamic-Glazed Pork Loin 84

Parmesan Pork Roast 86

Chinese Five-Spice Pork Ribs 88

Dijon Pork Chops with Apples 90

Rustic Rosemary-Apple Pork Roast 91

Coconut Pork Curry 92

Ginger + Clove-Spiked Pulled Pork 94

Honey Mustard-Glazed Ham 96

Ham and Potatoes 97

Apple Cider Pork Roast

Serves: 10
Time: 7-8 hours, 15 minutes (5 minutes prep time, 7-8 hours cook time, 10 minutes rest time)

A recipe large enough to feed ten of your favorite friends and family, this pork roast is sweetened with organic apple cider and sweet onion, and spiced with smoked paprika, ginger, and chili powder. In a slow cooker, you never have to worry about underdone pork, and the cider-based sauce ensures the meat is melt-in-your-mouth tender.

Ingredients:

5-pounds boneless pork butt
1 peeled and sliced sweet onion
1 ½ cups unsweetened organic apple cider
1 tablespoon sea salt
1 ½ teaspoons garlic powder
1 ½ teaspoons smoked paprika
½ teaspoon ground ginger
½ teaspoon chili powder
½ teaspoon black pepper

Directions:

1. Mix all the ground spices together in a bowl.
2. Rub pork evenly with spices.
3. Put onion slices in the slow cooker and add roast on top.
4. Pour over cider.
5. Cook on high for 7-8 hours.
6. Remove pork and plate to cool for a few minutes.
7. Pour cooking liquid through a sieve back into the pot.
8. When pork is rested, shred and put back into the pot.
9. Coat in the cooking liquid and season with more salt and pepper if necessary.
10. Serve!

Nutritional Info (1/10 recipe per serving):
Total calories: 442
Protein: 40
Carbs: 1
Fat: 28
Fiber: 0

Pork Carnitas

Serves: 6
Time: 4-6 hours, 10 minutes (5 minutes prep time, 4-6 hours cook time, 5 minutes broil time)

One of my favorite kinds of taco is a taco with pork carnitas, or slow-cooked shredded pork. The meat is rubbed in a mixture of spices like chili powder and cumin, and cooked in the slow cooker with onion, lime, and jalapeno. After it's done, I like to just quickly pick out any big hunks of fat, and then broil the pork for just 5 minutes to get tasty little crispy edges!

Note: If the pork is really thick, you'll cook it at or close to the full 6 hours. Pork should be served at 145-degrees.

Ingredients:

4 pounds boneless pork shoulder
Juice of 2 limes
1 sliced onion
1 seeded and diced jalapeno pepper
1 tablespoon olive oil
1 tablespoon chili powder
1 teaspoon salt
1 teaspoon ground cumin
½ teaspoon black pepper

Directions:

1. Pat the pork shoulder dry with paper towels.
2. In a bowl, mix dry spices and then rub into the meat.
3. Put meat in the slow cooker.
4. Pour over olive oil and then add jalapeno and onions.
5. Squeeze in lime juice and close the lid.
6. Cook on low for 4-6 hours.
7. Shred the pork, picking out any especially big hunks of fat.
8. Spread shredded pork on a cookie sheet and stick under

the broiler for 5 minutes to get crispy.
9. Serve in tacos, over salad, or as a sandwich!

Nutritional Info (⅙ recipe per serving):
Total calories: 501
Protein: 82
Carbs: 3
Fat: 16
Fiber: 0

CHAPTER 10: PORK

Balsamic-Glazed Pork Loin

Serves: 4
Time: 6-8 hours, 5 minutes (5 minutes prep time, 6-8 hours cook time)

Balsamic vinegar is like the wine of vinegars. The older the better, both in flavor and nutrition. Because a little goes a long way, I totally recommend investing in a really good balsamic that you know is all-natural. That balsamic is going to be the base of a glaze that goes on your pork loin, which cooks in the slow cooker with sage, salt, pepper, garlic, and stock. The pork would be delicious served just like that, but the balsamic glaze with a little coconut sugar and soy sauce takes the meat to new heights.

Ingredients:

3 pounds boneless pork loin
½ cup water
½ cup organic chicken broth
½ cup coconut sugar
¼ cup organic balsamic vinegar
2 tablespoons soy sauce
1 tablespoon cornstarch
1 minced garlic clove
1 teaspoon ground sage
½ teaspoon salt
½ teaspoon black pepper

Directions:

1. Mix sage, salt, pepper, and garlic in a bowl.
2. Rub evenly unto the pork.
3. Put roast in the slow cooker and pour in ½ cup chicken stock.
4. Cook on low for 6-8 hours.
5. When the slow cooker is nearly done, whisk water, sugar, soy sauce, balsamic vinegar, and cornstarch together in a

saucepan.
6. Slowly bring to a boil and then reduce the heat to simmer.
7. Glaze should thicken in 2-3 minutes.
8. Shred pork and then drizzle over the balsamic glaze before serving.

Nutritional Info (¼ recipe per serving):
Total calories: 603
Protein: 71
Carbs: 35
Fat: 27
Fiber: 0

CHAPTER 10: PORK

Parmesan Pork Roast

Serves: 4-6
Time: 6-7 hours, 15 minutes (5 minutes prep time, 6-7 hours cook time, 10 minutes gravy time)

Parmesan cheese is one of the few ingredients in the world naturally-rich in "umami," which has been called the "fifth taste." Basically, parmesan cheese has that flavor that makes you go "wow" when you taste it. That "wow" is the base of the gravy that cooks with a boneless pork roast for 6-7 hours in a slow cooker. The other ingredients - basil, garlic, soy sauce, honey - all serve to complement and accentuate that parmesan. Because the cheese is so important, spring for a good hard parmesan, and not something that comes in a bag.

Ingredients:

2-3 pounds boneless pork roast
⅔ cups grated Parmesan cheese
½ cup honey
¼ cup cold water
3 tablespoons soy sauce
2 tablespoons cornstarch
2 tablespoons dried basil
2 tablespoons minced garlic
2 tablespoons olive oil
½ teaspoon salt

Directions:

1. Grease slow cooker with a coconut-oil based cooking spray.
2. Put roast in your slow cooker.
3. Mix cheese, honey, soy sauce, garlic, oil, basil, and salt in a bowl.
4. Pour over pork and close the lid.
5. Cook overnight for 6-7 hours.
6. When ready, move the pork and rest on a plate.

7. Skim fat from the top of the cooking liquid.
8. Pour cooking liquid into a saucepan and bring to a boil.
9. In a cup, mix water and cornstarch until smooth.
10. Pour into the saucepan and bring to a boil again.
11. Stir for 2 minutes to thicken.
12. Serve roast with gravy!

Nutritional Info (264 grams per serving):
Total calories: 607
Protein: 57.8
Carbs: 33.3
Fat: 26.5
Fiber: 0

Chinese Five-Spice Pork Ribs

Serves: 6
Time: 8-10 hours, 21 minutes (6 minutes prep time, 8-10 hours cook time, 15 minutes additional time)

Chinese five-spice seasoning is underused in America, and it's a real shame, because it's amazing. Made from Szechuan peppercorns, cloves, star anise, cinnamon, and fennel, it transforms ordinary baby back ribs into something special. The sauce in this recipe shouldn't be ignored either; it's coconut aminos, rice vinegar, and tomato paste, so it's salty, sweet, and savory. The ribs cook for 8-10 hours, and then broil for 10 minutes. Don't forget to drizzle on the sauce before digging in!

Ingredients:

4 pounds baby back ribs
1 fresh jalapeno
2 tablespoons coconut aminos
2 tablespoons rice vinegar
1 tablespoon organic tomato paste
2 teaspoons Chinese five-spice seasoning
¾ teaspoons garlic powder
Salt and black pepper to taste

Directions:

1. Cut ribs so they will fit standing up in your slow cooker.
2. Season with salt, pepper, garlic powder, and Chinese five-spice.
3. Cut jalapeno into rings and then add to the bottom of the slow cooker.
4. Pour in coconut aminos, rice vinegar, and tomato paste.
5. Stir until the paste has dissolved.
6. Arrange the ribs so they're standing up in the cooker; this way, they aren't submerged in the liquid.
7. Cook 8-10 hours on low if you want to cook them

overnight.
8. When the cooker is done, take out the ribs.
9. Skim fat off the top and pour liquid into a saucepan.
10. Bring to a boil, and then simmer.
11. For crispy ribs, finish them off for 10 minutes in a 400-degree oven.
12. Drizzle sauce on ribs before serving.

Nutritional Info (⅙ recipe per serving):
Total calories: 631
Protein: 48
Carbs: 2
Fat: 48
Fiber: 0

Dijon Pork Chops with Apples

Serves: 4
Time: 5-6 hours, 5 minutes (5 minutes prep time, 5-6 hours cook time)

By mixing Dijon mustard, honey, salt, and pepper and pouring over apples, onion, and pork chops, you're creating an amazing honey-mustard sauce that brings spicy-sweetness to your boneless chops. After 5-6 hours, those flavors are sealed into the meat, so every bite is more delicious than the last.

Ingredients:

1 ½ pounds boneless pork chops
5 peeled and sliced apples
1 sliced onion
3 tablespoons organic honey
1 teaspoon Dijon mustard
½ teaspoon salt
Black pepper to taste

Directions:

1. Put pork chops into your slow cooker.
2. In a bowl, mix honey, Dijon, salt, and pepper.
3. Put apples and onions in your slow cooker, and pour the sauce over everything.
4. Cook on high for 5-6 hours.
5. Serve right away!

Nutritional Info (¼ recipe per serving):
Total calories: 341
Protein: 32
Carbs: 42
Fat: 3
Fiber: 5.5

Rustic Rosemary-Apple Pork Roast

Serves: 4
Time: 8-10 hours

What are "rustic" flavors like? Think "rich, "roasted," "deep," and "earthy." In this recipe, "rustic" takes the form of fresh herbs like rosemary and basil, fresh apples with their skin, chives, and sea salt. A pork shoulder roast cooks in those ingredients with bone broth for 8-10 hours on low, getting that deep-roasted flavor you'll love.

Ingredients:

3-pounds pork shoulder roast
1 cup chicken bone broth
6 sprigs fresh rosemary
4 fresh basil leaves
3 chopped apples, skin-on
1 tablespoon chopped chives
½ teaspoon sea salt
¼ teaspoon black pepper

Directions:

1. Add all the ingredients into your slow cooker and close the lid.
2. Cook overnight on low for 8-10 hours.
3. Slice the roast before serving!

Nutritional Info (¼ recipe per serving):
Total calories: 697
Protein: 64
Carbs: 16
Fat: 37
Fiber: 3.2

Coconut Pork Curry

Serves: 6
Time: 4 hours, 15 minutes (15 minutes prep time, 4 hours cook time)

I love pork and coconut together. Both are slightly nutty and slightly sweet, and the fat of the coconut milk keeps the meat moist as they cook for 4 hours on high. To cut through the sweetness, you'll use fresh ginger, onion, garlic, and spices like turmeric and curry powder. You can choose the level of heat you want in your curry by choosing a mild or spicy curry powder.

Ingredients:

4 pounds cubed boneless pork shoulder
One 14-ounce can of diced tomatoes
2 cups chicken stock
1 cup full-fat coconut milk
1 chopped onion
3 tablespoons minced fresh ginger
2 tablespoons coconut oil
3 minced garlic cloves
1 tablespoon ground cumin
1 tablespoon curry powder
½ teaspoon turmeric
Salt and pepper to taste

Directions:

1. In a skillet, heat coconut oil.
2. When hot, add pork and brown.
3. Season with salt and pepper before moving to slow cooker.
4. Add garlic, ginger, onion, curry powder, cumin, and turmeric to the skillet, making sure there's still some fat left.
5. Cook on low until the onion has softened.
6. Add this into your slow cooker, along with the tomatoes,

stock, and coconut milk.
7. Cook on high for 4 hours.
8. Skim fat off the surface of the cooking liquid.
9. Serve with brown rice!

Nutritional Info (⅛ recipe per serving):
Total calories: 802
Protein: 62
Carbs: 10
Fat: 57
Fiber: 1

Ginger + Clove-Spiked Pulled Pork

Serves: 6
Time: 8 hours, 5 minutes (5 minutes prep time, 8 hours cook time)

Ginger and clove are the two strongest spices in this pulled pork, but there's also thyme, cumin, garlic and sweet paprika. The spiced pork is cooked in apple cider, which gives it a lip-smacking sweetness, for 8 hours. It's a great meal to make overnight and serve at a BBQ or picnic.

Ingredients:

3 pounds boneless pork butt
1 bay leaf
1 cup unsweetened organic apple cider
1 tablespoon garlic powder
2 teaspoons grated fresh ginger
1 ½ teaspoons ground clove
1 ½ teaspoons ground thyme
1 teaspoon sweet paprika
1 teaspoon salt
½ teaspoon cumin

Directions;

1. Mix all the dry spices together.
2. Rub all over the pork.
3. Put in the slow cooker, the fatty side up, and pour over the apple cider.
4. Add bay leaf and close the lid.
5. Cook on low for 8 hours.
6. When time is up, take out the pork and shred.
7. Mix meat with a few tablespoons of the cooking liquid.
8. Mix in your favorite organic BBQ sauce before serving!

Nutritional Info (⅙ recipe per serving):
Total calories: 445
Protein: 40
Carbs: 1
Fat: 28
Fiber: 0

Honey Mustard-Glazed Ham

Serves: 6-8
Time: 4-6 hours, 5 minutes (5 minutes prep time, 4-6 hours cook time)

The honey-mustard glaze on this spiral ham is unique, thanks to the little bit of cloves. It helps bridge the gap between the spicy Dijon and sweet honey. When you're choosing a ham, always go with organic, without nitrates or antibiotics. Pure Farms is a good choice.

Note: The ham cooks for 4-6 hours, and you'll want to baste it every 2 hours to keep it from drying out.

Ingredients:

1 organic spiral-sliced, cooked ham (120-ounces)
½ cup organic honey
¼ cup water
2 tablespoons Dijon mustard
¼ teaspoon ground cloves

Directions:

1. Put ham in your slow cooker.
2. In a saucepan, mix honey, cloves, mustard, and water.
3. Cook on high until the honey has dissolved and is fully incorporated into mustard.
4. Pour over the ham and close the lid.
5. Cook on high for 4-6 hours, basting with its own cooking juice every 2 hours.
6. Serve hot!

Nutritional Info (⅙ recipe per serving):
Total calories: 952   Fat: 47
Protein: 87   Fiber: 0
Carbs: 36

Ham and Potatoes

Serves: 6
Time: 6 hours, 5 minutes (5 minutes prep time, 6 hours cook time)

Have some leftover ham? This hearty recipe is down-to-earth and oh-so delicious. It's got that ham, green beans, potatoes, and cheese. For the cream of chicken soup, go with an organic brand like Pacifica. It has ingredients like creme fraiche, water, rice flour, and other natural ingredients. This soup is mixed with a little milk, onion powder, salt, and pepper, and then poured over the potatoes, ham, onion, green beans, and cheese. Cook for 6 hours on low, and add more cheese before enjoying!

Ingredients:

One (10.75-ounce) container of organic cream of chicken soup
5 cups sliced russet potatoes
3 cups green beans
2 cups diced cooked organic ham
2 cups shredded cheddar cheese
½ cup diced onion
⅓ cup whole organic milk
½ teaspoon onion powder
¼ teaspoon salt
¼ teaspoon black pepper

Directions:

1. In a bowl, mix soup, milk, onion powder, salt, and pepper.
2. Add green beans, potatoes, ham, onion, and 1 cup of cheese to your slow cooker.
3. Pour over the sauce.
4. Stir and then flatten everything down with a spatula.
5. Cook on low for 6 hours.
6. When it's ready, sprinkle on remaining cheese.
7. When melted, serve!

Nutritional Info (⅙ recipe per serving):
Total calories: 359
Protein: 30
Carbs: 33
Fat: 16
Fiber: 4.5

Chapter 11 - Seafood

Seafood is one of those proteins that are different from any other. The flavor profile from fish to fish can be very diverse, but they're all great vehicles for spices like citrus, herbs, peppers. This section is packed with succulent, healthy seafood like tilapia packets, Asian-inspired salmons, and creamy chowders. When you're buying seafood, always try to go with what's in season, and stay updated on any warnings about mercury or other heavy metals. Unless you only eat seafood (which is rare; honestly, most us really should eat more fish), you don't really need to worry about metals if you're eating more than one kind of fish.

Mandarin-Orange Tilapia *100*

Hearty Seafood Stew *101*

Tilapia + Asparagus Packets *103*

Tomato-Rosemary Cod *104*

Asian Salmon Stir-Fry *106*

Maple Salmon *107*

Coconut-Milk White Fish *108*

Shrimp Scampi *109*

Shrimp Risotto *110*

Seafood Gumbo *112*

Tuna-Mushroom Casserole *114*

Salmon Chowder *116*

Clam Chowder *118*

CHAPTER 11: SEAFOOD

Mandarin-Orange Tilapia

Serves: 4
Time: 2 hours, 5 minutes (5 minutes prep time, 2 hours cook time)

With only six ingredients, you can make a dinner for four that's light and bright with citrus flavors and garlic. Tilapia is one of my favorite white fish, and it doesn't hurt that it's super cheap, too. To cook fish in a slow cooker, you're going to wrap the fillet in foil, with the garlic, butter, oranges, salt, and pepper inside. After 2 hours, the fish should be cooked to perfection.

Ingredients:

One 10-ounce can of drained organic mandarin oranges
4 tilapia filets
2 tablespoons melted butter
2 teaspoons garlic powder
Salt and pepper to taste

Directions:

1. Lay out a piece of aluminum foil, large enough to fit all four fish fillets.
2. Lay them down side by side in the center of the foil, and pour on butter.
3. Sprinkle garlic powder on fish evenly.
4. Take a handful of oranges and lay them on each fillet.
5. Finish off with a sprinkle of salt and pepper.
6. Fold over the foil and seal the edges, creating a fish packet.
7. Put in your slow cooker and cook on high for 2 hours.
8. Be careful removing the packet, and serve!

Nutritional Info (¼ recipe per serving):
Total calories: 167   Fat: 7
Protein: 21   Fiber: 1
Carbs: 7

Hearty Seafood Stew

Serves: 6-8
Time: 4 hours, 30-45 minutes

Aromatic and rich, seafood stew is a great way to eat a lot of fish at once. This recipe uses just cod and clams, with veggies like celery, onion, and tomatoes. The seafood actually doesn't need to go in the slow cooker until after everything else has cooked for 4 hours on high; the fish and clams go in for just 30-45 minutes.

Ingredients:

1 pound chopped cod filets
One 28-ounce can diced tomatoes
One 6 ½-ounce can undrained + chopped clams
2 cups chopped onion
2 chopped celery stalks
½ cup dry white wine
¼ cup chopped parsley
1 tablespoon red wine vinegar
1 tablespoon olive oil
5 minced garlic cloves
2 ½ teaspoons lemon-pepper seasoning
¼ teaspoon coconut sugar
¼ teaspoon crushed red pepper flakes

Directions:

1. Put all ingredients except clams and cod in the slow cooker.
2. Cook for four hours on high.
3. When it's ready, add in your seafood and cook for another 30-45 minutes, until the fish is flaky and has a solid color.
4. Serve with oyster crackers!

Nutritional Info (⅙ recipe per serving):
Total calories: 193
Protein: 22
Carbs: 15
Fat: 3
Fiber: 3

Tilapia + Asparagus Packets

Serves: 4
Time: 2 hours, 5 minutes (5 minutes prep time, 2 hours cook time)

This recipe gives you an entree and a side in one easy package. The tilapia is seasoned simply with just lemon juice, lemon pepper seasoning, and butter, and wrapped in foil with asparagus. When you have four packets, cook in the slow cooker for just 2 hours on high.

Ingredients:

4 thawed tilapia fillets
8-12 tablespoons lemon juice
1 bundle asparagus
2 tablespoons butter
Sprinkle of lemon pepper seasoning

Directions:

1. Cut a piece of foil for each fillet and divide up the asparagus evenly.
2. With the fillet on the foil, season with lemon pepper seasoning, lemon juice, and butter.
3. Top with asparagus and fold over the foil, sealing the ends together.
4. Cook on high for 2 hours.
5. When time is up, carefully unwrap the packets and enjoy!

Nutritional Info (¼ recipe per serving):
Total calories: 165
Protein: 21
Carbs: 3
Fat: 8
Fiber: 2.7

CHAPTER 11: SEAFOOD

Tomato-Rosemary Cod

Serves: 4
Time: 35 minutes (5 minutes prep time, 30 minutes cook time)

This is a very fast slow cooker recipe; it only takes 35 minutes total! Everything goes in the slow cooker at once - cod, diced tomatoes, stock, bell pepper, onion, garlic, and seasonings. After 35 minutes on high, the fish and veggies are ready. This is a meal that's great in the summer, because it's fresh, and the cooker isn't on long enough to heat up your kitchen.

Ingredients:

1 pound cod
One 15-ounce can of diced tomatoes
¼ cup chicken stock
1 sliced bell pepper
1 sliced onion
3 minced garlic cloves
1 tablespoon dried rosemary
¼ teaspoon red pepper flakes
¼ teaspoon salt
¼ teaspoon black pepper

Directions:

1. Pour broth, tomatoes, garlic, rosemary, and seasonings into your slow cooker.
2. Layer on onion and bell pepper, and stir.
3. Season fish with more salt and pepper, and put in the cooker.
4. Cook on high for just 30 minutes.
5. Serve with the tomato mixture on top!

Nutritional Info (¼ recipe per serving):
Total calories: 128
Protein: 20
Carbs: 11
Fat: 1
Fiber: 4.2

CHAPTER 11: SEAFOOD

Asian Salmon Stir-Fry

Serves: 4
Time: 2-3 hours

Don't bother buying a bunch of vegetables for this recipe, just get a package of frozen Asian stir-fry vegetables, which include carrots, broccoli, and baby corn. The salmon and veggies are cooked with a simple sauce of honey, soy sauce, and lemon juice. For a full meal, serve with cooked brown rice.

Ingredients:

12-ounces of frozen Asian stir-fry vegetable blend
10-ounces salmon fillets
2 tablespoons honey
2 tablespoons soy sauce
2 tablespoons lemon juice
Salt and pepper to taste

Directions:

1. Discard the sauce packet from the vegetables.
2. Pour vegetables into the slow cooker.
3. Season salmon with salt and pepper.
4. Put on top of the vegetables.
5. In a bowl, mix honey, soy sauce, and lemon juice.
6. Pour over the salmon and veggies, and close the slow cooker lid.
7. Cook on low for 2-3 hours. If you like your salmon well-done, go the full 3 hours.
8. Serve fish with cooking liquid and with brown rice.

Nutritional Info (¼ recipe per serving):
Total calories: 199   Fat: 10
Protein: 15   Fiber: 2
Carbs: 11

Maple Salmon

Serves: 6
Time: 60 minutes

The previous salmon recipe used honey - this one uses maple syrup in the sauce, along with lime juice, soy sauce, garlic, and ginger. Pour this over your salmon and cook for one hour on high. That's it! It's a slow cooker recipe you can make after work from frozen fish.

Ingredients:

6 frozen wild-caught salmon fillets
½ cup pure maple syrup
¼ cup organic soy sauce
⅛ cup lime juice
2 teaspoons crushed garlic
1 teaspoon minced ginger root

Directions:

1. Put salmon in your slow cooker.
2. In a bowl, mix the rest of the ingredients and pour over fish.
3. Cook on high for 1 hour.
4. Serve!

Nutritional Info (⅙ recipe per serving):
Total calories: 236
Protein: 25
Carbs: 20
Fat: 7
Fiber: 0

CHAPTER 11: SEAFOOD

Coconut-Milk White Fish

Serves: 4
Time: 1 hour, 5 minutes (5 minutes prep time, 60 minutes cook time)

Fragrant and light, this fish recipe can be adapted with any aromatics of your choice. I like to use a simple mixture of garlic and fresh ginger, which cuts through the rich coconut milk poaching liquid beautifully, adding a contrast of flavors. For a full meal, serve with a vegetable side, like riced cauliflower with salt and pepper.

Ingredients:

4 white fish fillets
½ can of organic full-fat coconut milk
3 minced garlic cloves
1 teaspoon minced fresh ginger
Salt to taste
Hot water

Directions:

1. Put fish in your slow cooker, so the skin is facing down.
2. Sprinkle in garlic, ginger, and salt.
3. Heat coconut milk on the stovetop until it's simmering.
4. Pour over fish.
5. Add enough hot water so all the fillets are submerged.
6. Cook on high for 1 hour.
7. Serve with fresh parsley!

Nutritional Info (¼ recipe per serving):
Total calories: 283
Protein: 42
Carbs: 2
Fat: 11
Fiber: 0

Shrimp Scampi

Serves: 4
Time: 1 ½ hours

Shrimp scampi can be prepared a lot of ways, and in this recipe, you'll be focusing on just the shrimp part. Make sure to get raw shrimp, and thaw it before adding it to the slow cooker with white wine, stock, oil, parsley, and garlic. The seafood only needs to cook for 1 ½ hours. You'll know the shrimp is done when it's a bright, solid pink. Serve as is with sauce on top, or with brown rice or whole-wheat pasta.

Ingredients:

1 pound thawed raw shrimp
½ cup white wine
¼ cup organic chicken stock
2 tablespoons olive oil
2 teaspoons minced parsley
2 teaspoons minced garlic
Salt and pepper to taste

Directions:

1. Mix stock, wine, lemon juice, olive oil, parsley, and garlic in your slow cooker.
2. Add thawed shrimp and close the lid.
3. Cook on high for 1 ½ hours.
4. Serve with the shrimp in a bowl, with sauce poured over it!

Nutritional Info (¼ recipe per serving):
Total calories: 161
Protein: 16
Carbs: 1
Fat: 8
Fiber: 0

Shrimp Risotto

Serves: 4
Time: 2 ½ hours

Risotto on the stovetop is a laborious process. In the slow cooker, all you have to do is put in the ingredients, and let it go! You cook the shrimp separately in a skillet, which only takes a few minutes. The risotto is more of a porridge than a traditional risotto, but it's full of savory, addicting flavors everyone will love.

Ingredients:

1 pound shelled and cleaned shrimp
3 ¾ cups organic chicken stock
1 ¼ cups Arborio rice
½ cup chopped onions
½ cup grass-fed butter
½ cup shredded Parmesan cheese
¼ cup white wine
3 minced garlic cloves
1 tablespoon olive oil
Salt and pepper to taste

Directions:

1. Add rice, broth, garlic, and butter to your slow cooker.
2. Cook for 2 ½ hours on low.
3. When there's 10 minutes left or so, heat olive oil in a skillet and add shrimp.
4. Cook on both sides until nearly cooked through.
5. Pour in wine and cook until the shrimp is solid and pink.
6. When the slow cooker is ready, stir in shrimp.
7. Add cheese and let it melt.
8. Season with salt and pepper before serving!

Nutritional Info (¼ recipe per serving):
Total calories: 587
Protein: 25
Carbs: 49
Fat: 32
Fiber: 0

Seafood Gumbo

Serves: 6-8
Time: 3-4 hours

Gumbo takes me to New Orleans, where spirits and spices are high. This recipe uses all the best stew ingredients, like chicken thighs, shrimp, sausage, aromatics, and of course, cajun seasoning. Everything but the shrimp goes in the slow cooker and cooks for 3-4 hours. For really rich flavors, I recommend going the full four. When there's 20 minutes or so left, add raw shrimp.

Ingredients:

3 pounds organic boneless, skinless chicken thighs
1 pound thawed shrimp
One 15-ounce can of diced tomatoes
½ pound chopped organic pork sausage
4 minced garlic cloves
2 diced celery stalks
1 diced bell pepper
1 diced onion
1 cup frozen okra
6-ounces organic tomato paste
2 tablespoons cajun seasoning
1 bay leaf
½ teaspoon salt
½ teaspoon black pepper

Directions:

1. Put everything except the shrimp into your slow cooker.
2. Cook on high for 3-4 hours.
3. When there's about 20 minutes left, add shrimp and finish cooking.
4. Pick out the bay leaf and serve hot!

Nutritional Info (⅙ recipe per serving):
Total calories: 568
Protein: 72
Carbs: 13
Fat: 25
Fiber: 2.3

CHAPTER 11: SEAFOOD

Tuna-Mushroom Casserole

Serves: 4-6
Time: 3 hours, 5 minutes (5 minutes prep time, 3 hours cook time)

Tuna casserole is classic comfort food. Packed with both tuna and veggies like peas, carrots, and onion, it warms the soul and body. The casserole is lightened up a bit in this recipe, and replaces pasta with fresh mushrooms and the sour cream with coconut milk. The final result is creamy, cheesy, and comforting.

Ingredients:

3 cans of tuna fish
1 pound chopped fresh button mushrooms
2 cans of organic cream of mushroom soup
1 can of organic full-fat coconut milk
2 cups water
1 cup shredded cheddar cheese
⅓ bag of frozen peas and carrots
¼ diced onion
Salt and pepper to taste

Directions:

1. Drain one can of tuna and scrape into the slow cooker.
2. Pour in the other two cans, with their juices, into the cooker.
3. Pour in soup, water, and coconut milk.
4. Stir.
5. Add onion, mushrooms, and frozen veggies.
6. Season well with salt and pepper, and then stir again before closing the lid.
7. Cook for 3 hours on high.
8. When time is up, add cheese and close the lid, just so the cheese can melt.
9. Season to taste again if necessary, and enjoy!

Nutritional Info (¼ recipe per serving):
Total calories: 488
Protein: 32
Carbs: 24
Fat: 30
Fiber: 2.25

Salmon Chowder

Serves: 4
Time: 4 hours, 15 minutes

You know clam chowder, but what about salmon chowder? It's a good alternative for people who don't like clams. The chowder is creamy, savory, and rich with buttery red potatoes and corn. Using seafood stock instead of chicken stock ensures the natural flavors of salmon come through strong.

Note: The chowder is also a great way to use leftover salmon. You just need about 1 cup of cooked salmon if you opt for that over canned salmon. If you are getting canned salmon, make sure it says "wild" on it.

Ingredients:

One 24-ounce can of drained corn
Two 5-ounce cans of drained wild-caught salmon
8-ounces diced red potatoes
2 cups organic seafood stock
1 cup heavy cream
1 diced onion
1 seeded and diced red bell pepper
1 teaspoon seafood seasoning
Salt and pepper to taste
Hot sauce to taste

Directions:

1. Put potatoes, corn, onion, pepper, stock, and seasoning in your slow cooker.
2. Cook on high for 3-4 hours.
3. When you're about 15 minutes away from serving, pour half of the liquid into a blender and puree.
4. Pour back into the cooker with the cream, salmon, and hot sauce.

5. Stir, and then cook for another 15 minutes.
6. Taste and season again if necessary.

Nutritional Info (¼ recipe per serving):
Total calories: 287
Protein: 21
Carbs: 45
Fat: 5
Fiber: 6.5

Clam Chowder

Serves: 4-6
Time: 3 hours, 30 minutes

A New England classic, clam chowder is very easy to make in your slow cooker. I like using coconut milk instead of cream, in case anyone is sensitive to dairy, and lots of bacon. Aromatics like onion and carrots bring a lot of depth to the chowder, while flour allows you to get that beautiful, thicker chowder texture.

Note: When shopping for minced clams, look for words like "organic" and "natural," and always read the ingredient list. Bar Harbor All Natural is a good brand.

Ingredients:

Two 6.5-ounce cans of minced clams
Two 12-ounce cans of full-fat coconut milk
1 ⅓ cups water
½ cup organic seafood stock
6 slices cooked organic bacon
2 peeled and diced potatoes
3 chopped and peeled carrots
1 chopped onion
¼ cup whole-wheat flour
1 teaspoon organic Worcestershire sauce
½ teaspoon salt
½ teaspoon black pepper

Directions:

1. Pour stock, water, onion, carrots, and potatoes into the slow cooker
2. Cook on high for 3 hours.
3. In a bowl, mix flour and ½ cup coconut milk until smooth.
4. Pour into cooker along with clams and the rest of the milk.
5. Stir well before cooking for another 30 minutes on high.

6. Crumble bacon.
7. Top soup with bacon, and season with more salt and pepper if necessary before serving!

Nutritional Info (¼ recipe per serving):
Total calories: 612
Protein: 15
Carbs: 38
Fat: 44
Fiber: 5.2

Chapter 12 - Sides + Snacks

The perfect side dish can really complete a meal. They're also a great way to get in really healthy ingredients like vegetables and whole grains. Certain side dishes can even be eaten as snacks, like this section's recipe for spiced chickpeas or jalapeno cornbread! If you are assigned the sides for this year's big holiday gathering, you are sure to find a recipe here that will impress everyone, but not take too much work on your part.

Mashed Cauliflower with Garlic + Herbs *121*

Garlic-Herb Mushrooms *123*

Spiced Chickpeas *125*

Beans + Rice *126*

Macaroni and Cheese *127*

Applesauce Sweet Potatoes *128*

Creamed Corn *129*

Butternut Squash with Apples and Cranberries *130*

Rosemary-Honey Beets *131*

Wild Rice Stuffing *133*

Pear + Sausage Stuffing *135*

Sweet Potato Casserole *137*

Jalapeno Cornbread *139*

Mashed Cauliflower with Garlic + Herbs

Serves: 4
Time: 3 hours, 5 minutes (3 hours cook time, 5 minutes blend time)

Mashed cauliflower instead of mashed potatoes is a great substitute for those interested in getting more vegetables, and you can't even really tell the difference. Lots of garlic, fresh herbs, and butter help, of course. Cook the cauliflower for 3 hours, and then mash or puree to your preferred texture. Don't be afraid of seasoning - like potatoes, cauliflower doesn't have much flavor on its own, so spice away.

Ingredients:

4-6 cups water
1 big cauliflower's worth of florets
6 peeled, whole garlic cloves
1 cup organic veggie broth
4 tablespoons minced rosemary, sage, and thyme
3 tablespoons grass-fed butter
Salt and black pepper to taste

Directions:

1. Put cauliflower in the slow cooker.
2. Add garlic, vegetable broth, and just enough water to cover the florets.
3. Cook on high for 3 hours.
4. Drain and return the cauliflower to the cooker.
5. Add butter and mash well. You can also move to a blender and puree if you like.
6. Season with herbs, salt, and pepper.

Nutritional Info (¼ recipe per serving):
Total calories: 134
Protein: 6
Carbs: 10
Fat: 9
Fiber: 5

Garlic-Herb Mushrooms

Serves: 4
Time: 3-4 hours, 5 minutes (3-4 hours cook time, 5 minutes warm time)

Mushrooms are one of my favorite bite-sized appetizers, and this recipe shows you why. The mushrooms are cooked with just garlic, herbs, and stock, and then mixed with creamy coconut milk and seasoned with lots of salt and pepper. It's almost like you've made yourself a little stew, and even though it's just one ingredient, the mushrooms never get boring.

Ingredients:

24-ounces cremini mushrooms
1 bay leaf
1 cup organic vegetable broth
¼ cup full-fat coconut milk
4 minced garlic cloves
2 tablespoons grass-fed butter
2 tablespoons minced parsley
½ teaspoon dried oregano
½ teaspoon dried basil
¼ teaspoon dried thyme
Salt and pepper to taste

Directions:

1. Add mushroom, herbs, and garlic to your slow cooker.
2. Pour in broth.
3. Cook on low for 3-4 hours.
4. When time is up, pour in coconut milk and stir.
5. Keep the cooker on till the milk is warm.
6. Pick out the bay leaf.
7. Season to taste with salt and pepper.
8. Serve!

CHAPTER 12: SIDES + SNACKS

Nutritional Info (¼ recipe per serving):
Total calories: 126
Protein: 6
Carbs: 8
Fat: 9
Fiber: 1.9

Spiced Chickpeas

Serves: 8
Time: 5 hours

Chickpeas are incredibly healthy, but bland on their own. That's why you need to add a myriad of flavors. I like using Ras el Hanout, which is a traditional Moroccan seasoning blend. You can get it just about anywhere. It has cumin, ginger, black pepper, cayenne, and more. You're also going to add a red onion and your favorite fresh herbs. After 5 hours, the chickpeas are ready to serve as is or mixed in another dish.

Ingredients:

3 ½ cups water
2 cups dried chickpeas
2 cups canned diced tomatoes
½ cup fresh herbs
1 diced red onion
2 tablespoons Moroccan seasoning (Ras el Hanout)

Directions:

1. Before putting chickpeas in your cooker, pick through them and remove any stones.
2. Rinse.
3. Put in the cooker with water, onion, and spice mix.
4. Cook on high for 4 hours.
5. When time is up, add tomatoes (with their juice) and cook for another hour.
6. Season more if necessary.
7. Garnish with herbs before serving!

Nutritional Info (⅛ recipe per serving):
Total calories: 200   Fat: 3
Protein: 10   Fiber: 9
Carbs: 34

Beans + Rice

Serves: 6
Time: 2-3 hours

When you need an easy side dish for a Mexican entree, this is the perfect go-to. You're going to be using pre-cooked beans to cut down on time. Be sure to get a good brand that has as few ingredients as possible. All canned beans need are the beans and salt. Mix the beans and brown rice in your cooker with fresh tomatoes and butter, and some essential seasonings like cumin and garlic. Cook for just 2-3 hours on high, and it's ready!

Ingredients:

3 cups rinsed and drained cooked black beans
2 cups water
1 ½ cups fresh diced heirloom tomatoes
1 cup dry brown rice
1 tablespoon grass-fed melted butter
1 teaspoon cumin
½ teaspoon garlic powder
Salt to taste
Hot sauce to taste

Directions:

1. Mix rice and butter in your slow cooker.
2. Add beans.
3. Add the rest of the ingredients and stir.
4. Cook on high for 2-3 hours.
5. When rice is cooked, season more to taste if necessary and serve!

Nutritional Info (⅙ recipe per serving):
Total calories: 178   Fat: 3
Protein: 9   Fiber: 9.5
Carbs: 32

Macaroni and Cheese

Serves: 8
Time: 5 hours

This classic Southern side dish can be eaten as a snack or even a meal on its own. We're going with whole-wheat macaroni noodles, and cooking them in organic milk with cheese, eggs, and seasonings. The result is the cheesy, creamy, dreamy mac and cheese kids and adults alike dream about.

Ingredients:

½ pound uncooked whole-wheat macaroni noodles
3 cups whole organic milk
3 cups shredded Cheddar cheese
2 organic eggs
1 teaspoon garlic salt
½ teaspoon mustard powder
½ teaspoon black pepper

Directions:

1. Keep ½ cup cheese on the side.
2. Add the rest of the ingredients to the cooker.
3. Cook on low for 5 hours.
4. Add rest of the cheese on top.
5. When melted, eat!

Nutritional Info (⅛ recipe per serving):
Total calories: 314
Protein: 19
Carbs: 24
Fat: 17
Fiber: 1.2

CHAPTER 12: SIDES + SNACKS

Applesauce Sweet Potatoes

Serves: 8
Time: 6-8 hours, 5 minutes (5 minutes prep time, 6-8 hours cook time)

For a simple sweet potato side dish, all you need is the sweet potatoes, applesauce, butter, and cinnamon! The applesauce gives the potatoes a creamy texture that's just a little bit sweet, as well as a subtle cider-like flavor that is perfect for the autumn season. Cinnamon adds just a bit of spice that keeps every bite as interesting and tasty as the last.

Ingredients:

7 cubed organic sweet potatoes
1 cup unsweetened, natural applesauce
3 tablespoons grass-fed melted butter
1 ½ teaspoons cinnamon

Directions:

1. Put sweet potato cubes in your slow cooker.
2. In a bowl, mix butter, cinnamon, and applesauce.
3. Pour sauce over the potatoes and close the lid.
4. Cook on low for 6-8 hours.
5. When time is up, mash to your desired texture.
6. Serve!

Nutritional Info (⅛ recipe per serving):
Total calories: 156
Protein: 2
Carbs: 26
Fat: 4
Fiber: 3.3

Creamed Corn

Serves: 6
Time: 2-4 hours

Creamed corn is a common dish for holidays like Thanksgiving, and we've lightened it up a bit for this recipe. Instead of the usual cream cheese, we're using organic coconut cream. If you're worried the corn will taste too "coconut-ty," don't worry, because the flavor is mild enough to be masked by salt and pepper. The coconut cream even adds a bit of its own sweetness, so you don't need to add any sweeteners.

Ingredients:

16-ounces frozen corn
8-ounces organic coconut cream
½ cup whole organic milk
½ cup grass-fed butter
Salt and pepper to taste

Directions:

1. Mix corn, cream, milk, and butter in your slow cooker.
2. Cook on high for 2-4 hours.
3. When time is up, stir well and season with salt and pepper.
4. Serve!

Nutritional Info (⅙ recipe per serving):
Total calories: 284
Protein: 3
Carbs: 10
Fat: 26
Fiber: 1.5

Butternut Squash with Apples and Cranberries

Serves: 6
Time: 4 hours

If you know me, you know that I'm a huge fan of butternut squash. It's one of the most naturally-sweet vegetables out there, and the texture is simply divine. This side dish is diced butternut squash with apples, dried cranberries, and of course, butternut squash's favorite seasonings - cinnamon and nutmeg.

Ingredients:

3 pounds peeled, seeded, and diced butternut squash
4 peeled, cored, and diced sweet apples
¾ cup unsweetened dried cranberries
½ diced white onion
1 tablespoon cinnamon
1 ½ teaspoons nutmeg

Directions:

1. Mix all the ingredients in your slow cooker.
2. Cook on high for 4 hours.
3. When time is up, taste and season with a little salt if necessary.

Nutritional Info (⅙ recipe per serving):
Total calories: 229
Protein: 3
Carbs: 58
Fat: 0
Fiber: 6.7

Rosemary-Honey Beets

Serves: 12
Time: 7-8 hours, 10 minutes (10 minutes prep time, 7-8 hours cook time)

There are a lot of people who don't like beets, but that's only because they haven't seen what it is possible with fresh beets and a slow cooker. You're going to cook three pounds of beets in a cooker with tangy balsamic vinegar, sweet honey, rosemary, garlic, salt, and black pepper. They all work so well together, and after 7-8 hours, the beets are infused with addicting and delicious flavor even the naysayers will love.

Ingredients:

3 pounds beets
⅓ cup honey
¼ cup white balsamic vinegar
2 tablespoons olive oil
1 tablespoon chopped rosemary leaves
2 chopped garlic cloves
Salt and pepper to taste

Directions:

1. Spray your cooker with a coconut-oil based spray.
2. Cut the tops of the beets, and peel.
3. Put in the slow cooker.
4. In a bowl, mix vinegar, honey, oil, rosemary, garlic, salt, and pepper.
5. Pour over the beets and close the lid.
6. Cook on low for 7-8 hours.
7. When time is up, slice beets into rounds and serve!

CHAPTER 12: SIDES + SNACKS

Nutritional Info (1/12 recipe per serving):
Total calories: 100
Protein: 2
Carbs: 20
Fat: 2.5
Fiber: 3

Wild Rice Stuffing

Serves: 20
Time: 1 hour, 10 minutes (30 minutes prep time, 40 minutes cook time)

Wild rice is one of the healthiest types of rice out there, and full of nutty, earthy flavor. For this stuffing that can feed a massive crowd, you'll be using wild rice and tasty ingredients like dried cranberries, pine nuts, water chestnuts, apricots, and green onion. You're going to cook the rice part-way on the stove, and then add it to the slow cooker with the rest of the ingredients for 40 minutes on low.

Ingredients:

9 cups organic chicken stock
4 cups raw wild rice
3 cups cubed French bread
1 diced onion
1 diced organic green apple
One 8-ounce can drained sliced water chestnuts
4 minced garlic cloves
1 ½ cups chopped celery
¾ cup pine nuts
¾ cup dried unsweetened cranberries
¾ cup chopped walnuts
½ cup chopped dried apricots

Directions:

1. In a saucepan, bring 8 cups of chicken broth and rice to a boil.
2. Reduce and simmer for a half hour.
3. Pour into the cooker with remaining 1 cup of broth and rest of the ingredients.
4. Cook on low for 40 minutes, or until the wild rice has split and is soft.

Nutritional Info (1/20 recipe per serving):
Total calories: 243
Protein: 9
Carbs: 34
Fat: 7
Fiber: 2.5

Pear + Sausage Stuffing

Serves: 10
Time: 3-4 hours, 15 minutes (15 minute prep time, 3-4 hours cook time)

Tired of the same old stuffing? This version is a bit unique, and uses fresh pears in addition to the usual dried cranberries, bread, and seasonings. The meat is pork sausage, so you can eat this stuffing right out of a bowl by itself if you crave it. The bread doesn't have to be stale, you're going to be toasting it in the oven for just 15 minutes before adding to the rest of the ingredients.

Ingredients:

24-ounces pork sausage
10-12 cups dry bread cubes
5 cored and diced organic pears
3 organic eggs
2 cups organic chicken stock
1 cup unsweetened dried cranberries
5 chopped celery stalks
1 chopped onion
4 tablespoons grass-fed butter
1 teaspoon dried sage
1 teaspoon poultry seasoning
Salt and pepper to taste

Directions:

1. To dry your bread, put cubes on a cookie sheet and bake in a 400-degree oven for 15 minutes.
2. While that bakes, you can brown your sausage in a skillet.
3. When it's brown, remove sausage.
4. Add butter to pan and add celery and onion.
5. Cook 8-10 minutes, until the onion has softened.
6. Return sausage and reduce heat to low.
7. In a bowl, mix bread cubes with seasonings, cranberries,

and pears.
8. Spoon in the sausage skillet and add to your slow cooker.
9. In another bowl, whisk stock and eggs together.
10. Pour into the slow cooker and mix.
11. Cook on low for 3-4 hours.

Nutritional Info (1/10 recipe per serving):
Total calories: 482
Protein: 13
Carbs: 19
Fat: 27
Fiber: 4

Sweet Potato Casserole

Serves: 6-8
Time: 3 hours, 5 minutes (5 minutes prep time, 3 hours cook time)

Sweet potato casserole is usually very sugary, but in this recipe, the only sugar you'll be using is 3 tablespoons of maple syrup. The topping is just toasted pecans and melted butter, and the natural sugars in the sweet potatoes are all you need for a delicious side dish. Cinnamon, orange zest, and nutmeg bring all those flavors together.

Ingredients:

5 medium organic sweet potatoes
2 beaten organic eggs
2 cups unsweetened coconut milk
¾ cup chopped toasted pecans
3 tablespoons pure maple syrup
2 tablespoons grass-fed melted butter
1 tablespoon orange zest
1 teaspoon cinnamon
½ teaspoon nutmeg

Directions:

1. Peel sweet potatoes and cube.
2. Put in the slow cooker and cover with the coconut milk.
3. Cook on high for 3 hours.
4. While that cooks, toast your pecans by spaying a cookie sheet with a coconut-based spray.
5. Arrange nuts on tray in a single layer, and put in a 350-degree oven.
6. Cook for just 5 minutes, keeping a close eye on them, so they don't burn.
7. When slow cooker is done, mash the potatoes.
8. Add in maple syrup, orange zest, cinnamon, and nutmeg.

9. Stir well.
10. In a separate bowl, mix pecans and butter.
11. Top potatoes with the buttered pecans.
12. Serve hot!

Nutritional Info (⅙ recipe per serving):
Total calories: 274
Protein: 5
Carbs: 28
Fat: 17
Fiber: 4.6

Jalapeno Cornbread

Serves: 12
Time: 1 hour, 11 minutes - 1 hour, 41 minutes (5 minutes prep time, 1-1 ½ hours cook time, 6 minutes cool time)

Bring some cornbread with a kick to your holiday table this year. Made with ingredients like Greek yogurt and whole-wheat flour, this cornbread is moist and full of flavor. A teaspoon of chili powder and sliced jalapenos on top add that touch of heat that will make this cornbread stand out.

Ingredients:

1 cup yellow cornmeal
1 cup whole-wheat flour
1 cup plain Greek yogurt
1 cup milk
1 egg
2 seeded and sliced jalapenos
3 tablespoons coconut sugar
2 tablespoons melted butter
4 teaspoons baking powder
1 teaspoon chili powder
1 teaspoon salt

Directions:

1. Put parchment paper in your slow cooker, so the bread is easier to take out.
2. Spray the sides, too, with a coconut-oil based spray.
3. In a bowl, mix flour, cornmeal, sugar, salt, chili powder, and baking powder.
4. In another bowl, mix your yogurt, milk, butter, and egg.
5. Mix the wet into the dry.
6. Pour into the cooker, topping with the sliced jalapenos.
7. Cook on high for 1-1 ½ hours.
8. When time is up, stick a toothpick in the center. If it comes

out mostly clean, it's ready!
9. Cool a little while before removing and serving.

Nutritional Info (1/12 recipe per serving):
Total calories: 147
Protein: 5
Carbs: 23
Fat: 4
Fiber: 2

Chapter 13 – Vegan

Vegan food can be so delicious that even non-vegans will want to dig in. This section has a breakfast oatmeal inspired by cake; chilis and soups full of flavor from ingredients like mango and butternut squash; and spaghetti squash and tofu lunch bowls that will make your mouth water. Don't forget about dessert, either! Whether you're a chocolate or fruit lover, there are two recipes that will satisfy that sweet tooth without any artificial ingredients.

Carrot + Zucchini Cake Oatmeal *142*

Perfect Vegetable Soup *143*

Black Bean + Mango Chili *145*

Butternut Squash + Bean Chili *147*

Spaghetti Squash + Broccoli Bowl with Peanut Dressing *148*

Lentil Stew with Polenta *150*

Pineapple-Teriyaki Tofu *152*

Braised Tofu *154*

Spiced Potatoes + Chickpeas *156*

Chocolate Pudding Cake *158*

Green Apple Crumble *160*

CHAPTER 13: VEGAN

Carrot + Zucchini Cake Oatmeal

Serves: 3
Time: 6-8 hours

A non-savory oatmeal with carrot and zucchini? Absolutely! These vegetables have a very subtle natural sweetness that's brought out by maple syrup, vanilla, and spices like nutmeg. You cook the steel-cut oats in almond milk with the veggies overnight, and then top with crunchy, buttery pecans in the morning!

Ingredients:

1 ½ cups unsweetened almond milk
½ cup steel-cut oats
¼ cup chopped pecans
1 small grated carrot
¼ small peeled and grated zucchini
2 tablespoons pure maple syrup
1 teaspoon pure vanilla extract
Pinch of nutmeg
Pinch of salt
Pinch of cinnamon

Directions:

1. Grease the inside of your slow cooker with a coconut-oil based spray.
2. Mix all the ingredients except pecans in the cooker and close the lid.
3. Cook overnight on low for 6-8 hours.
4. Stir and add pecans before serving!

Nutritional Info (⅓ recipe per serving):
Total calories: 233   Fat: 10
Protein: 4   Fiber: 1.6
Carbs: 31

Perfect Vegetable Soup

Serves: 4
Time: 3-5 hours

This is the perfect vegetable soup because it's so easy to make, takes less time than most slow cooker recipes, and is just as good reheated for lunch. It's got just about all my favorite vegetables, including sweet potato, green beans, bell pepper, tomatoes, and more. A bay leaf adds a lot of rustic savoriness, while seasoning with salt is all you need to do to bring out all the bright, fresh flavors.

Ingredients:

4 cups organic vegetable stock
3 cups diced tomatoes
3 chopped celery stalks
3 chopped carrots
1 peeled and diced sweet potato
1 diced sweet onion
1 cup halved green beans
1 chopped yellow bell pepper
3 minced garlic cloves
1 bay leaf
Salt to taste

Directions:

1. Put everything in your slow cooker and close the lid.
2. Cook on high for 3-5 hours until the veggies are softened to your liking.
3. Pick out the bay leaf.
4. Season with more salt if necessary before eating!

Nutritional Info (¼ recipe per serving):
Total calories: 138
Protein: 4
Carbs: 29
Fat: 0
Fiber: 7

Black Bean + Mango Chili

Serves: 4-6
Time: 8-10 hours, 10 minutes

Have you ever had mango in a chili? You're about to discover just how amazing it is. Mango is not a super-sweet fruit, so it adds just a little hint that's brought out by golden raisins and fresh orange juice. The hotter spices like smoked paprika, cumin, and a jalapeno balance out the chili, which takes 8-10 hours to cook. You add the mango for just the last ten minutes, and then serve!

Ingredients:

Two 14.5-ounce cans of fire-roasted tomatoes
4 cups cooked black beans
2 cups diced mango
2 cups diced yellow onion
½ cup fresh orange juice (no sugar added)
½ cup golden raisins
3 minced garlic cloves
1 diced jalapeno
1 tablespoon chili powder
1 teaspoon cumin
½ teaspoon smoked paprika
½ teaspoon cinnamon
Salt and pepper to taste

Directions:

1. Add everything minus the mangos to your slow cooker, and stir.
2. Cook overnight for 8-10 hours on low.
3. When done, add mango and cook on low for just 10 minutes.
4. Season with more salt and pepper if necessary.
5. Serve!

Nutritional Info (¼ recipe per serving):
Total calories: 500
Protein: 19
Carbs: 95
Fat: 6
Fiber: 20

Butternut Squash + Bean Chili

Serves: 4
Time: 3-4 hours

For a faster slow cooker recipe, I like to use packages of frozen vegetables. For this chili, you're going to use butternut squash. It doesn't even need to be thawed, so it's very convenient. Mix the squash with cooked black beans, tomatoes, garlic, and spices like chili powder and cocoa powder, and cook for just 3-4 hours on high.

Ingredients:

Two 15.5-ounce cans of cooked black beans
Two 14-ounce cans of diced tomatoes
10-ounce package of frozen butternut squash
4 minced garlic cloves
1 chopped red onion
1 cup water
1 tablespoon cumin
1 tablespoon chili powder
2 teaspoons unsweetened organic cocoa powder
¼ teaspoon cinnamon

Directions:

1. Mix everything in your slow cooker and close the lid.
2. Cook on high for 3-4 hours.
3. Serve hot!

Nutritional Info (¼ recipe per serving):
Total calories: 379
Protein: 23
Carbs: 72
Fat: 1
Fiber: 11.5

CHAPTER 13: VEGAN

Spaghetti Squash + Broccoli Bowl with Peanut Dressing

Serves: 2
Time: 2-3 hours, 20-30 minutes (2-3 hours cook time, 20-30 minutes cool time)

I love everything about this lunch bowl. Spaghetti squash is the most versatile vegetable I know, and goes so well with tender-steamed broccoli and the addicting homemade peanut dressing made from beautiful ingredients like fresh lime juice, garlic, and ginger. One bowl is less than 150 calories, with almost 6 grams of protein and over 7 grams of fiber!

Ingredients:

5-pounds spaghetti squash
2 cups water
2 cups steamed broccoli
1 batch of peanut dressing
1 tablespoon sesame seeds

Dressing:

¾ tablespoons coconut sugar
1 ½ tablespoons fresh lime juice
1 ½ tablespoons vegetable oil
½ tablespoon coconut aminos
1 minced garlic clove
1 tablespoon organic creamy peanut butter
½ tablespoon grated ginger
½ teaspoon sesame oil
Pinch of salt

Directions:

1. Poke the spaghetti squash all over with a fork.

2. Put whole, pierced squash in the cooker with 2 cups of water.
3. Cook on high for 2-3 hours.
4. Cool cooked squash for 20-30 minutes.
5. While that cools, prepare the dressing by whisking all the ingredients together.
6. Cut squash in half long-wise and remove seeds and pulp.
7. Shred flesh with a fork into "noodles."
8. Divide broccoli and noodles into two bowls, and drizzle on dressing.
9. Enjoy!

Nutritional Info (½ recipe per serving):
Total calories: 145.9
Protein: 5.6
Carbs: 26.4
Fat: 4.3
Fiber: 7.5

Lentil Stew with Polenta

Serves: 6
Time: 7 hours, 5 minutes (5 minutes prep time, 7 hours cook time)

Lentils are one of the best sources of protein and fiber for vegans. This recipe uses brown lentils, which cook in the slow cooker with onion, green bell peppers, garlic, sweet plum tomatoes, and spices. The polenta cooks separately on the stove, when the lentils are almost done. Serve the stew on top of the polenta.

Ingredients:

1 ½ cups brown lentils
1 ½ cups vegetable broth
One 28-ounce can of plum tomatoes
1 cup quick-cooking polenta
4 sliced garlic cloves
2 sliced onions
1 diced green bell pepper
1 tablespoon balsamic vinegar
1 teaspoon dried oregano
½ teaspoon salt
Pinch of crushed red chili flakes

Directions:

1. Put lentils, onion, bell pepper, and garlic in your slow cooker, in that order.
2. Cut the plum tomatoes in half and put in the cooker, pouring in their juice, as well.
3. Add seasonings.
4. Pour in vinegar and broth.
5. Cover and cook on low for 7 hours.
6. When the slow cooker is close to being done, follow the polenta box instructions on cooking.
7. Serve stew over the polenta.

Nutritional Info (⅙ recipe per serving):
Total calories: 300
Protein: 16
Carbs: 57
Fat: 1
Fiber: 15

CHAPTER 13: VEGAN

Pineapple-Teriyaki Tofu

Serves: 4
Time: 8-10 hours, 5 minutes (5 minutes prep time, 8-10 hours cook time)

Get a taste of the tropics with this tofu cooked in a sauce made from pineapple juice, coconut aminos, rice vinegar, garlic, ginger, and more. Even people who believe tofu is always bland will be converted, and want to keep eating more. Serve with brown rice for a full meal.

Ingredients:

2 pounds extra-firm tofu
6 pineapple rings
1 cup unsweetened 100% pineapple juice
½ cup organic vegetable broth
½ cup coconut aminos
¼ cup rice vinegar
4 minced garlic cloves
2 tablespoons coconut sugar
1 tablespoon fresh grated ginger
1 tablespoon sesame oil

Directions:

1. Drain tofu, and slice into 6 pieces.
2. Press down on them to remove extra cut.
3. Cut tofu pieces again, in half, and then again diagonally so you get little triangles.
4. In a bowl, mix pineapple juice, vegetable broth, vinegar, sugar, oil, ginger, garlic, and coconut aminos together.
5. Add pineapple and tofu into the slow cooker, and pour over the sauce.
6. Cook overnight on low for 8-10 hours.
7. Serve with brown rice!

Nutritional Info (¼ recipe per serving):
Total calories: 398
Protein: 23
Carbs: 47
Fat: 14
Fiber: 1

CHAPTER 13: VEGAN

Braised Tofu

Serves: 4
Time: 3 hours, 5 minutes (5 minutes prep time, 3 hours cook time)

The secret to this tofu's amazing flavor is the gochujang sauce. Gochujang is a fermented Korean red chili sauce that's spicy, sweet, and savory all at once. You don't need much else to make the tofu delicious, so we're going to be serving the tofu on a bed of baby spinach and sprinkle on some green onions. If you're extra-hungry, add brown rice.

Ingredients:

2 pounds extra-firm tofu
8-ounces baby spinach
4 sliced green onions
¼ cup gochujang sauce
¼ teaspoon salt

Directions:

1. Drain packages of tofu.
2. Wrap tofu in papers towels, and put on a plate.
3. Cover with another plate to squeeze out as much liquid as possible.
4. Unwrap tofu and cut into thin slices.
5. Put in the bottom of your slow cooker, ideally in a single layer.
6. Season with salt and pour in gochujang.
7. Cook on high for 3 hours.
8. Serve with spinach and green onions on top, and rice, if desired.

Nutritional Info (¼ recipe per serving/does not count rice):
Total calories: 290
Protein: 23
Carbs: 27
Fat: 12
Fiber: 6

CHAPTER 13: VEGAN

Spiced Potatoes + Chickpeas

Serves: 4-6
Time: 8-10 hours, 10 minutes (10 minutes prep time, 8-10 hours cook time)

This mixture of potatoes and canned chickpeas with cumin, ginger, coriander, and garam masala, an Indian spice mix, is very easy to make. There's a bit of skillet work to soften the onion, and then get the spices cooked with tomatoes, tomato paste, and broth. Once that's done, the potatoes and chickpeas cook in the spice mixture for 8-10 hours. Cook overnight and take to work for your lunch.

Ingredients:

Two 15-ounce cans of drained and rinsed chickpeas
1 pound diced red potatoes
One 15-ounce can of diced tomatoes
1 cup organic vegetable broth
1 diced yellow onion
2 minced garlic cloves
2 tablespoons organic tomato paste
2 teaspoons olive oil
2 teaspoons cumin
2 teaspoons coriander
½ teaspoon ground ginger
½ teaspoon garam masala
Pinch of red pepper flakes
Salt to taste
1 fresh lime

Directions:

1. Pour olive oil into a large skillet and heat.
2. Add onions and cook for 5 minutes, until softening.
3. Add garlic, cumin, coriander, ginger, red pepper flakes, and salt.

4. Cook and stir for another minute.
5. Add diced tomatoes, broth, and tomato paste.
6. Stir, and then pour into the slow cooker.
7. Add chickpeas and potatoes.
8. Close the lid.
9. Cook on LOW for 8-10 hours.
10. Serve with a squirt of fresh lime juice!

Nutritional Info (¼ recipe per serving):
Total calories: 357
Protein: 20
Carbs: 65
Fat: 4
Fiber: 18.7

Chocolate Pudding Cake

Serves: 6
Time: 2 hours, 36 minutes (6 minutes prep time, 2 hours cook time, 30 minutes rest time)

In whole food cooking, we try to avoid sweeteners of any kind, but when it comes to dessert, it's okay to cheat a little bit. You're going to be using coconut sugar in this recipe for a ooey-gooey chocolate pudding cake. You make a pudding batter, and then sprinkle the top with a mixture of cocoa and coconut sugar before pouring on hot water. Don't stir, because the hot water on top turns the cocoa and sugar into a sauce.

Ingredients:

1 ½ cups hot water
1 cup whole-wheat flour
1 ¼ cups coconut sugar
½ cup unsweetened soy milk
¼ cup + 2 tablespoons unsweetened organic cocoa
2 tablespoons vegetable oil
2 teaspoons baking powder
1 teaspoon vanilla
½ teaspoon salt

Directions:

1. Grease your slow cooker with a coconut-oil based spray.
2. Mix flour, ½ cup sugar, 2 tablespoons cocoa, salt, and baking powder in a bowl.
3. Stir in oil, vanilla, and milk.
4. Pour into the slow cooker.
5. In a separate bowl, mix in the rest of the sugar and ¼ cup cocoa.
6. Sprinkle this mixture over the batter in the slow cooker.
7. Pour in hot water, and DO NOT STIR.
8. Cook on high for 2 hours.

9. When done, take off the lid and wait 30 minutes.
10. Serve in bowls!

Nutritional Info (⅙ recipe per serving):
Total calories: 324
Protein: 5
Carbs: 67
Fat: 6
Fiber: 2.1

CHAPTER 13: VEGAN

Green Apple Crumble

Serves: 3
Time: 4 hours, 5 minutes (5 minutes prep time, 4 hours cook time)

Pure maple syrup is a decent whole food sweetener because it's less processed than normal sugar, but even then, it's best to use it in moderation. In this recipe, you only need ⅛ of a cup. The rest of the sweetness comes from the apples and organic apple juice. For the granola, choose one that's as organic as possible (if you don't make your own), with little to no added sugar. The Kind brand's Healthy Grains Granola Clusters have 9 grams of sugar per ½ cup, and that comes from dried cane and brown rice syrup.

Ingredients:

2 green apples
1 cup all-natural granola
¼ cup unsweetened organic apple juice
⅛ cup pure maple syrup
2 tablespoons vegan butter
1 teaspoon cinnamon
½ teaspoon nutmeg

Directions:

1. Peel, core, and cut apples into chunks.
2. Add to the slow cooker with the rest of the ingredients, and stir.
3. Cook on low for just 4 hours.
4. Serve hot!

Nutritional Info (⅓ recipe per serving/will vary based on granola brand):

Total calories: 369
Protein: 5
Carbs: 56

Fat: 15
Fiber: 5

Chapter 14 - Dips and Sauces

A slow cooker can make more than just meals. It can be used to create delicious dips for parties and homemade sauces that are way healthier and tastier than anything you can find in a jar. This section includes dip classics like spinach and artichoke, and pasta-ready sauces like garlic-basil tomato sauce and butternut squash sauce!

Cheesy Crab Dip 162

Spinach Artichoke Dip 163

Chorizo-Chipotle Bean Dip 165

10-Hour Chicken Stock 167

Homemade Pizza Sauce 169

Vegetable Marinara Sauce 171

Garlic-Basil Tomato Sauce 173

Sausage + Beef Meat Sauce 174

Butternut Squash Sauce 176

Cranberry Sauce 178

CHAPTER 14: DIPS AND SAUCES

Cheesy Crab Dip

Makes: 4 cups
Time: 3 hours

Do you love crab? Or dips in general? This unique crab dip combines lump crab meat, healthy cottage cheese, melty mozzarella, and bold flavors from jalapeno and stone-ground mustard for a dip that's sophisticated enough to serve before a dinner party, and so easy you just throw everything in your slow cooker at once.

Ingredients:

1 pound lump crab meat
4-ounces cottage cheese
2 cups shredded mozzarella cheese
1 seeded and diced red bell pepper
1 minced jalapeno pepper
2 minced garlic cloves
4 tablespoons fresh lemon juice
2 tablespoons organic Worcestershire sauce
½ teaspoon stone-ground mustard

Directions:

1. Mix everything in a bowl.
2. Grease your slow cooker with a coconut-oil based spray.
3. Pour dip contents into the slow cooker.
4. Cook on low for 3 hours.
5. When time is up, stir and enjoy!

Nutritional Info (1 cup per serving):
Total calories: 322
Protein: 45
Carbs: 6
Fat: 13
Fiber: 0

Spinach Artichoke Dip

Serves: 8-10
Time: 3 hours, 5 minutes (5 minutes prep time, 3 hours cook time)

Just about everyone loves spinach-artichoke dip, so you should know how to make it. In the slow cooker is the perfect cooking method, and involves blending a mixture of garlic, almond milk, lemon juice, mustard, salt, and pepper in a blender, and then mixing in artichoke, spinach, cheese, and water chestnuts. That cooks for 3 hours on LOW, and is polished off with organic mayo.

Ingredients:

Two 14-ounce cans of drained, rinsed, and chopped artichoke hearts
8-ounces thawed and squeezed frozen spinach
8-ounces diced drained and rinsed water chestnuts
1 cup unsweetened almond milk
1 cup mozzarella cheese
⅓ cup parmesan cheese
2 chopped garlic cloves
3 tablespoons organic mayo
2 tablespoons fresh lemon juice
2 teaspoons Dijon mustard
Salt and black pepper to taste

Directions:

1. Blend garlic, milk, lemon juice, mustard, black pepper, and a little salt in a blender until smooth.
2. Pour into the slow cooker.
3. Stir in artichoke, spinach, chestnuts, and cheese.
4. Cook on low for 3 hours.
5. When time is up, add mayo. If the dip needs more liquid, pour in a little more almond milk.
6. Season to taste with more salt and black pepper if needed.

7. Serve!

Nutritional Info (⅛ recipe per serving):
Total calories: 133
Protein: 7
Carbs: 13
Fat: 6
Fiber: 1.8

Chorizo-Chipotle Bean Dip

Serves: 10-12
Time: 2 hours, 12 minutes (12 minutes prep time, 2 hours cook time)

For a dip packed with protein, it's hard to beat this chorizo sausage and bean dip, with not one, but two kinds of beans. After browning the sausage with onion and garlic, the pinto beans are mashed in the slow cooker. The whole black beans, sausage, tomatoes, chipotle, and rest of the ingredients go on top in the cooker and cook for just 2 hours on high.

Ingredients:

8-ounces raw chorizo sausage, with casings removed
One 15-ounce can of rinsed and drained black beans
One 15-ounce can of rinsed and drained pinto beans
One 14.5-ounce can of diced tomatoes, with juice
½ cup shredded Monterey jack cheese
¼ cup fresh cilantro
1 chopped onion
2 minced garlic cloves
1 teaspoon chopped chipotle pepper in adobo sauce

Directions:

1. Heat a skillet on the stove and add sausage, onion, and garlic.
2. Cook and stir until sausage is brown, then pour into a bowl.
3. Add black beans, tomatoes, chipotle pepper, and cilantro, and mix with sausage/onion/garlic.
4. Add pinto beans to your slow cooker, and mash well.
5. Add contents of sausage bowl and sprinkle on cheese.
6. Cook on high for 2 hours.
7. Serve warm!

Nutritional Info (1/10 recipe per serving):
Total calories: 173
Protein: 10
Carbs: 18
Fat: 10
Fiber: 3.9

10-Hour Chicken Stock

Makes: About 9 cups*
Time: 8-10 hours

It isn't a dip or a sauce, but chicken stock is an essential pantry staple. Whenever you cook a whole chicken, save the carcass and bones, and make your own stock. Just add water, and aromatics like a bay leaf, celery, carrots, onion, and herbs. Cook overnight for 8-10 hours, and then strain.

Note: How much stock you make depends on the size of your cooker. For a 4-6 quart cooker, 9 cups is about right.

Ingredients:

Leftover chicken carcass and bones
1 bay leaf
1 chopped onion
1 chopped celery stalk
1 chopped carrot
1 sprig parsley
1 sprig thyme
Water

Directions:

1. Put stock bones in the cooker.
2. Add celery, carrot, onion, and herbs.
3. Fill crockpot with water, leaving around ½-inch on top.
4. Cook on low for 8-10 hours.
5. When ready, pour stock through a fine sieve and discard solids.
6. Store in the fridge for no longer than 5 days, or freeze for up to 6 months.

Nutritional Info (1 cup per serving):
Total calories: 86
Protein: 6
Carbs: 9
Fat: 3
Fiber: 0

Homemade Pizza Sauce

Makes: About 5 cups
Time: 4 hours

Pizza sauce can be full of artificial ingredients, and not much flavor. To solve this problem, make your own. You'll be amazed at the difference, especially when you use organic tomato sauce and paste. In 4 hours, you'll have enough sauce to dress five pizzas.

Ingredients:

One 15-ounce can organic tomato sauce
Four 6-ounce cans organic tomato paste
1 cup water
4 tablespoons Parmesan cheese
3 tablespoons olive oil
2 tablespoons Italian seasoning
1 tablespoon organic honey
1 teaspoon garlic powder
1 teaspoon salt
½ teaspoon black pepper

Directions:

1. Mix all ingredients (minus cheese) in the slow cooker and close.
2. Cook on low for 4 hours.
3. Every 45 minutes to an hour, open up the lid and stir, so nothing sticks to the bottom and burns.
4. When time is up, add cheese.
5. When melted, cool to room temperature and store in bags.
6. Use within 1-2 days after storing in the fridge, or freeze.

Nutritional Info (½ cup per serving):
Total calories: 111
Protein: 3
Carbs: 16
Fat: 5
Fiber: 0

Vegetable Marinara Sauce

Makes: 7 cups
Time: 8 hours, 5 minutes (8 hours cook time, 5 minutes blend time)

No one will know this sauce is hiding two cups of chopped eggplant, which is a controversial vegetable in terms of who likes it and who hates it. The eggplant is secondary to the rich, warm flavors of whole tomatoes, garlic, and dried herbs. This is a very low-sugar sauce, and only has 1 teaspoon of coconut sugar.

Ingredients:

Two 28-ounce cans of whole tomatoes
2 cups peeled and chopped eggplant
1 bay leaf
5 peeled and chopped garlic cloves
1 chopped onion
1 ½ tablespoons Italian seasoning
1 tablespoon organic pesto
1 teaspoon organic coconut sugar
1 teaspoon salt
½ teaspoon dried rosemary
½ teaspoon dried thyme
Black pepper to taste

Directions:

1. Add everything to your slow cooker and cover.
2. Cook for 8 hours on low.
3. When time is up, open the cooker and pick out the bay leaves.
4. Puree in a blender until you get your desired texture.
5. Taste and season with more salt and pepper if needed.
6. Store in the fridge for up to 5 days, or freeze for up to 6 months.

Nutritional Info (½ cup per serving):
Total calories: 74
Protein: 3
Carbs: 14
Fat: 1
Fiber: 1.2

Garlic-Basil Tomato Sauce

Makes: 6 (enough for 1 pound of pasta)
Time: 4 hours, 6 minutes (6 minutes prep time, 4 hours cook time)

Garlic and basil are "must-have" flavors for any Italian dish, so this sauce can be used for just about anything from that region. You can also adjust the amount of dried basil and garlic to your liking; in the recipe, it's on the low side, so it isn't overpowering. Cooking the garlic beforehand helps bring out its flavor, too, so don't skip that part.

Ingredients:

One 28-ounce jar of canned whole tomatoes
3 tablespoons olive oil
2 teaspoons dried basil
2 teaspoons chopped garlic
Salt and pepper to taste

Directions:

1. Add olive oil to a skillet and heat.
2. Cook garlic until golden and fragrant.
3. Scrape into slow cooker and add tomatoes, olive oil, basil, salt, and pepper.
4. Stir and close the lid.
5. Cook on high for 4 hours.
6. When done, cool to room temperature before storing in a fridge for up to 5 days. If serving right away, no need to cool. To keep the sauce longer, freeze for up to 6 months.

Nutritional Info (⅙ recipe per serving):
Total calories: 89   Fat: 1
Protein: 1   Fiber: 1.6
Carbs: 6

CHAPTER 14: DIPS AND SAUCES

Sausage + Beef Meat Sauce

Serves: 8
Time: 8 hours, 20 minutes (20 minutes prep time, 8 hours cook time)

A good meat sauce is a "must-know" for any home chef. This recipe uses both beef and sausage, as well as diced and stewed tomatoes, and tomato sauce and tomato paste. Always go with organic to get the best flavors, and grass-fed meats. Cook on low for 8 hours to really let the flavors blend and deepen.

Ingredients:

1 pound grass-fed ground beef
¼ pound Italian sausage
One 14.5-ounce can Italian-style diced tomatoes
One 14.5-ounce can Italian-style stewed tomatoes
One 29-ounce can of tomato sauce
One 6-ounce can of tomato paste
2 chopped onions
2 tablespoons olive oil
1 tablespoon coconut sugar
1 teaspoon Italian seasoning
1 teaspoon garlic powder
Salt and pepper to taste

Directions:

1. Heat olive oil in a skillet and add onions and sausage.
2. Cook and stir for 10 minutes, until sausage is brown.
3. Add to slow cooker.
4. Add ground beef to skillet and brown with the Italian seasoning and garlic powder.
5. After 10 minutes, move to slow cooker.
6. Pour in the rest of the ingredients (minus sugar) and cook on low for 8 hours.
7. When there's 15 minutes left, add sugar.

8. Serve right away, or store in the fridge for up to 5 days, or in the freezer for up to 6 months.

Nutritional Info (⅛ recipe per serving):
Total calories: 264
Protein: 15
Carbs: 18.8
Fat: 14.8
Fiber: 3.7

CHAPTER 14: DIPS AND SAUCES

Butternut Squash Sauce

Serves: 7 cups
Time: 8 hours, 5 minutes (5 minutes prep time, 8 hours cook time)

Using butternut squash in this sauce is a great way to add in natural sweetness without any sugar. The squash is also great for texture, since you'll be pureeing the sauce at the end of the recipe. The rest of the sauce is made from fresh Roma tomatoes, garlic, bell peppers, and lots of seasonings. You can play with the dried spices to get the flavor you want, and even add more red pepper if you like a spicy sauce.

Ingredients:

4 cups peeled and diced butternut squash
4 halved garlic cloves
9 chopped Roma tomatoes
2 chopped red bell peppers
1 ¼ cups organic veggie broth
⅔ cup red wine
1 diced onion
2 tablespoons olive oil
1 tablespoon dried oregano
2 teaspoons salt
1 teaspoon dried rosemary
1 teaspoon crushed red pepper flakes
½ teaspoon black pepper

Directions:

1. Put all the veggies in your cooker.
2. In a bowl, mix wine, broth, and olive oil.
3. Mix in salt, herbs, pepper, and red pepper.
4. Pour over veggies and close the lid.
5. Cook on low for 8 hours.
6. When done, puree the veggies, adding vegetable broth as

needed to get the right texture.
7. Taste, and season with more salt and pepper if you think it needs it.
8. Serve over pasta!

Nutritional Info (1/7 recipe per serving):
Total calories: 134
Protein: 3
Carbs: 20
Fat: 4
Fiber: 4.8

CHAPTER 14: DIPS AND SAUCES

Cranberry Sauce

Serves: 4
Time: 7-8 hours, 40 minutes (7-8 hours cook time, 40 minutes cool time)

Every Thanksgiving spread includes cranberry sauce. If you don't want to spend forever boiling and babysitting the stove, make it in the slow cooker! You'll just need to add fresh cranberries, water, fresh orange juice, and some coconut sugar to the pot, and cook on low overnight. When the cranberries are hot, popped open, and bubbling, add in a generous sprinkle of orange zest. If the sauce looks thin, don't worry; it thickens as it cools.

Ingredients:

12-ounces fresh cranberries
½ cup water
½ cup fresh orange juice
⅓ cup coconut sugar
Sprinkle of orange zest

Directions:

1. Add everything (except zest) to your slow cooker.
2. Cook on low for 7-8 hours.
3. You'll know the sauce is done when the cranberries are all popped open, and the pot is bubbling.
4. Add zest.
5. As sauce cools, it thickens up. Cool to room temperature before serving or storing for up to 5 days in the fridge.

Nutritional Info (¼ recipe per serving):
Total calories: 101   Fat: 0
Protein: 0   Fiber: 0
Carbs: 27

Chapter 15 - Desserts

If you have a sweet tooth, dessert can be the best part of the meal. However, you want it to be as healthy as possible, and free from artificial ingredients and excess sugar. These desserts bear that in mind, and only include sweeteners when necessary, and instead rely on fresh fruit and spices like cinnamon and vanilla to create mouthwatering flavors. In this section, you'll be treated to desserts like oatmeal brimming with tart cherries, stuffed apples, poached pears, and more!

Cherry + Almond Dessert Oatmeal 180

Molten Lava Cake 181

Maple Créme Brûlée 183

Lemon Pudding Cake 185

Chai-Spiced Pears 187

Cranberry-Walnut Bread Pudding 188

Almond Banana Bread 190

Coconut Cream + Almond Butter-Stuffed Apples 192

Maple-Roasted Pear Crumble 194

Cocoa-Roasted Almonds 196

CHAPTER 15: DESSERTS

Cherry + Almond Dessert Oatmeal

Serves: 7
Time: 7 hours

Oatmeal doesn't have to be just for breakfast. This steel-cut oat dessert is cooked in vanilla almond milk, studded with dried tart cherries, and sweetened with applesauce. The almond extract and a drizzle of honey at the end also help give the oatmeal a sweet, rich dessert flavor.

Ingredients:

2 cups vanilla almond milk
1 ½ cups water
1 cup steel-cut oats
¾ cup dried tart cherries
½ cup unsweetened organic applesauce
1 tablespoon ground flax seed
½ teaspoon pure almond extract
Pinch of salt
Drizzle of organic honey

Directions:

1. Grease your slow cooker with a coconut-oil based spray.
2. Add everything to the cooker except honey and cover.
3. Cook on low for 7 hours.
4. When time is up, divide into bowls, drizzle each with honey, and serve!
5. Leftovers can go in the fridge, and even freeze if necessary.

Nutritional Info (1/7 recipe per serving/does not count honey):
Total calories: 186
Protein: 3
Carbs: 32
Fat: 3
Fiber: 3.2

Molten Lava Cake

Serves: 12

Time: 1 hour, 35 minutes - 2 hours, 5 minutes (5 minutes prep time, 1 ½-2 hours cook time)

Use your entire slow cooker to make a molten lava cake big enough to serve 12 people! The cake part is made with ingredients like oat flour, coconut sugar, coconut milk, and butter. For the cocoa powder, you want a high-quality, unsweetened, organic cocoa. It ensures the cake and sauce are both really rich and luxurious. The cake is made in layers, with the cake part going in the cooker first, followed by a sprinkling of coconut sugar and cocoa powder, and boiling water and honey on top of that. Do NOT stir. The last two layers create the sauce, which sinks to the bottom to make the molten part.

Ingredients:

Cake:
2 cups oat flour
1 ½ cups organic coconut sugar
1 cup unsweetened coconut milk
6 tablespoons organic cocoa powder
4 tablespoons grass-fed melted butter
1 tablespoon baking powder
2 teaspoons vanilla
1 teaspoon salt

Sauce:
2 cups boiling water
¾ cup organic coconut sugar
½ cup organic cocoa powder
¼ cup organic honey

Directions:

1. Grease a slow cooker with a coconut-oil based cooker.
2. In a bowl, look to the cake ingredients and whisk flour, cocoa, sugar, salt, and baking powder together.
3. Add in melted butter, vanilla, and coconut milk until smooth.
4. Pour into the slow cooker.
5. In another bowl, looking to the sauce list, mix cocoa powder and sugar.
6. Sprinkle over cake batter.
7. In a third bowl, mix honey and boiling water.
8. Pour over cake WITHOUT mixing, and cover lid.
9. Cook on high for 1 ½-2 hours.
10. You can tell the cake is done when it's puffed up and firm on top, with the sauce having sunk to the bottom.
11. Serve warm!

Nutritional Info (1/12 recipe per serving):
Total calories: 317
Protein: 5
Carbs: 65
Fat: 7
Fiber: 1.4

Maple Créme Brûlée

Serves: 3

Time: 6 hours, 25 minutes - 6 hours, 55 minutes (15 minutes prep time, 2-2 ½ hours cook time, 10 minutes cool time, 4 hours refrigerator time)

When you're ready to treat yourself, this créme brûlée is something special. The créme part has all the making's of the classic, but with pure organic maple extract added in for a more complex, breathtaking twist. The topping is just coconut sugar, which you should add and caramelize right before you serve.

Ingredients:

Créme:
Boiling water
1 ⅓ cups heavy whipping cream
3 egg yolks
½ cup coconut sugar
½ teaspoon pure organic maple extract
¼ teaspoon cinnamon

Topping:
3 teaspoons coconut sugar

Directions:

1. In a saucepan, heat cream until the sides begin to gently bubble on the sides.
2. While that is getting hot, whisk eggs yolks, sugar, and cinnamon together.
3. When the cream is forming bubbles on the side, remove from heat.
4. Stir a little of this hot cream into the yolks.
5. Pour yolks into the pan and whisk constantly to integrate.

6. Add maple.
7. Move créme into 6-ounces ramekins.
8. Put in your slow cooker and pour in one inches' worth of boiling water.
9. Cook on high for 2 -2 ½ hours until the ramekins jiggle, but the center is set.
10. Cool for 10 minutes outside of the cooker before wrapping in saran wrap and refrigerating for 4 hours.
11. When you're ready to eat, add 1 teaspoon of sugar per ramekin on top, and brulee with a torch.
12. Enjoy!

Nutritional Info (⅓ recipe per serving):
Total calories: 578
Protein: 5
Carbs: 44
Fat: 44
Fiber: 0

Lemon Pudding Cake

Serves: 4
Time: 2 hours, 16 minutes (6 minutes prep time, 2 hours cook time, 10 minutes cool time)

Light, bright, and only 216 calories per serving, this is a pudding cake lemon lovers will adore. It's very simple - plain Greek yogurt, two egg yolks, two egg whites, coconut sugar, flour, lemon juice and zest, and salt. The dry ingredients are added into the wet, with beaten, stiff-peaked egg whites added into the batter last, and then poured into ramekins. The cakes cook in the slow cooker with water for just two hours on low.

Ingredients:

⅔ cup plain Greek yogurt
2 egg yolks
2 egg whites
½ cup coconut sugar
¼ cup flour
1 lemon's worth of juice and zest
¼ teaspoon salt
Water

Directions:

1. Grease four 6-ounce ramekins.
2. In a bowl, whisk flour, salt, and sugar.
3. In another bowl, mix egg yolks, yogurt, lemon juice, and lemon zest.
4. When smooth, add dry ingredients into wet, until just mixed.
5. In another bowl, beat the egg whites until you get stiff peaks.
6. Fold whites into the batter.
7. Divide batter into the ramekins and set in your slow cooker.

8. Pour in just enough water to reach the halfway mark.
9. Close lid and cook on low for 2 hours.
10. Cool for 10 minutes before serving!

Nutritional Info (¼ recipe per serving):
Total calories: 216
Protein: 6
Carbs: 35
Fat: 6
Fiber: 0

Chai-Spiced Pears

Serves: 4
Time: 3-4 hours, 5 minutes (5 minutes prep time, 3-4 hours cook time)

Chai is my favorite flavor blends in the world. It's hard to beat sweet and spicy all at once. In this recipe, you're using real whole spices like cardamom pods, a cinnamon stick, and fresh peeled ginger. Fresh Bosc pears are cooked in orange juice with the spices and maple syrup, and basted every hour for 3-4 hours. If you want the pears really soft, with no bite, go for the full four.

Ingredients:

4 Bosc pears
2 cups fresh orange juice
5 whole cardamom pods
¼ cup pure maple syrup
1-inch piece of sliced peeled ginger
1 halved cinnamon stick

Directions:

1. Peel pears and cut off the bottom, so it stands up in the cooker.
2. Carefully remove the cores without destroying the fruit.
3. Put pears in the cooker, standing up.
4. Add the rest of the ingredients, spooning some juice over the top of the pears.
5. Cook on low for 3-4 hours, basting again with liquid every hour.
6. When the pears are soft, they're done!

Nutritional Info (¼ recipe per serving):

Total calories: 253   Fat: 1
Protein: 2   Fiber: 5.5
Carbs: 61

Cranberry-Walnut Bread Pudding

Serves: 6
Time: 4 hours, 10 minutes (10 minutes prep time, 4 hours cook time)

Bread soaked in a milk mixture, and dotted with tart dried cranberries and buttery walnuts, is a true comfort-food dessert. The sweetness comes from maple syrup, vanilla, and cinnamon. When the pudding is cooked, pour over a simple sauce of brown butter, which pulls those nutty, sweet flavors all together.

Ingredients:

5 cups cubed whole-wheat (or whole-grain) bread
2 ½ cups whole organic milk
3 beaten organic eggs
½ cup unsweetened dried cranberries
½ cup chopped walnuts
½ cup pure maple syrup
½ cup grass-fed butter
1 teaspoon pure vanilla extract
Dash of cinnamon

Directions:

1. In a bowl, whisk milk, eggs, syrup, cinnamon, and vanilla together.
2. Add bread and press it down, so it`s submerged.
3. Soak for 10 minutes.
4. In the meantime, grease your slow cooker with a coconut-oil based spray.
5. When 10 minutes has passed, add nuts and cranberries to the pudding.
6. Pour into the slow cooker.
7. Cook for 4 hours on low.
8. When there's about 10 minutes left on the slow cooker, add butter to a saucepan.

9. Cook on medium, stirring every once and while, to get brown butter. The butter will become aromatic, like a caramel, and get an amber color.
10. When the bread pudding is done and you're ready to serve, pour butter evenly on six servings.

Nutritional Info (⅙ recipe per serving):
Total calories: 488
Protein: 8
Carbs: 35
Fat: 26
Fiber: 2

Almond Banana Bread

Serves: 6
Time: 4 hours, 20 minutes (10 minutes prep time, 4 hours cook time, 10 minutes cool time)

When you have overripe bananas, what is there to do but make banana bread? This recipe embraces almonds, by adding sliced nuts and almond extract. I love the more intense flavors that almond extract brings over vanilla, and the crunch of the nuts adds contrast to the softness of the slow-cooked bread. Don't forget spices! Cinnamon, nutmeg, and a little salt are all you need.

Ingredients:

3 mashed bananas
2 cups whole-wheat flour
2 organic eggs
1 cup organic coconut sugar
¾ cup sliced almonds
½ cup grass-fed softened butter
1 teaspoon baking powder
1 teaspoon pure almond extract
½ teaspoon baking soda
½ teaspoon salt
¼ teaspoon cinnamon
⅛ teaspoon nutmeg

Directions:

1. Grease your slow cooker with a coconut-oil based spray.
2. In a large bowl, mix sugar, eggs, butter, and almond extract.
3. Add in baking soda, baking powder, salt, nutmeg, and cinnamon.
4. Stir in flour.
5. Stir in your mashed bananas and almonds.
6. Move batter to your slow cooker and cover with 3 paper

towels.
7. Close the lid.
8. Cook for 4 hours on LOW.
9. When time is up, carefully turn the slow cooker pot upside down on a plate to remove bread.
10. Serve at room temperature or cold!

Nutritional Info (⅛ recipe per serving):
Total calories: 570
Protein: 11
Carbs: 85
Fat: 23
Fiber: 8

CHAPTER 15: DESSERTS

Coconut Cream + Almond Butter-Stuffed Apples

Serves: 4
Time: 2-3 hours, 5 minutes (5 minutes prep time, 2-3 hours cook time)

Apples were designed to be cooked and stuffed with more goodness. In this recipe, the stuffing is coconut cream, natural almond butter, nutmeg, cinnamon, and salt. On top, a sprinkle of shredded coconut. Cook for 2-3 hours. This dessert has no sweeteners and is perfect for autumn, when apples are in season.

Ingredients:

4 cored green apples
1 cup water
4 tablespoons unsweetened shredded coconut
½ cup organic coconut cream
¼ cup unsweetened all-natural almond butter
2 tablespoons cinnamon
Pinch of salt
Pinch of nutmeg

Directions:

1. In a bowl, mix coconut cream, almond butter, nutmeg, cinnamon, and salt.
2. Put apples in your slow cooker with water.
3. Spoon coconut cream mixture into the hollowed apples.
4. Sprinkle on more cinnamon and shredded coconut.
5. Close the lid.
6. Cook for 2-3 hours on LOW. 3 hours results in very soft apples.
7. Serve hot!

Nutritional Info (¼ *recipe per serving*):
Total calories: 307
Protein: 5
Carbs: 31
Fat: 19
Fiber: 4.4

CHAPTER 15: DESSERTS

Maple-Roasted Pear Crumble

Serves: 6
Time: 5 hours, 30 minutes (5 hours cook time, 30 minutes oven time)

You've probably had apple crumble, but what about pear crumble? Six Bosc pears, my favorite, are cooked in a mixture of water, maple syrup, and spices for 4 hours on low. They get really soft and infused with sweetness, cinnamon, and ginger. Move to a baking dish, and top with the crumble made from rolled oats, coconut sugar, coconut oil, and more maple syrup. That cooks in an oven for another half-hour, until the crumble is golden and the sugars have caramelized.

Ingredients:

6 firm Bosc pears, cut in half
½ cup water
¼ cup pure maple syrup
1 teaspoon pure vanilla extract
1 teaspoon cinnamon
½ teaspoon ginger
¼ teaspoon nutmeg

Crumble:
⅔ cups rolled oats
2 tablespoons organic coconut sugar
1 tablespoon pure maple syrup
1 tablespoon coconut oil

Directions:

1. Put all the ingredients in the first list in the slow cooker.
2. Cook on high for one hour, and then switch to low for 4 hours.
3. When done, put pears and some cooking liquid in an 8x8 baking dish.

4. To make the crumble, pulse the ingredients in the second list in a food processor, until oats are sticky.
5. Sprinkle topping on pears and bake in a 350-degree oven for a half hour.
6. Serve!

Nutritional Info (⅙ recipe per serving):
Total calories: 260
Protein: 2
Carbs: 57
Fat: 3
Fiber: 1.5

CHAPTER 15: DESSERTS

Cocoa-Roasted Almonds

Makes: 2 cups
Time: 1 hour, 30 minutes

Need a dessert fix on the go? These whole almonds are slow-cooked in coconut sugar, cocoa, vanilla, and a dash of salt, with chopped butter pats on top. After an hour, you spread out the nuts to cool on a cookie sheet, and when they're cool, they're like little chocolatey jewels you can pop in your mouth for a rich, tiny treat.

Ingredients:

2 cups whole almonds
2 tablespoons grass-fed chopped butter
⅓ cup organic coconut sugar
1 tablespoon organic cocoa powder
1 teaspoon pure vanilla extract
Dash of salt

Directions:

1. Mix nuts, vanilla, sugar, cocoa, and salt in your slow cooker, with the butter on top.
2. Close the lid.
3. Cook on high for 60 minutes.
4. When done, open the lid, stir, and close the lid again.
5. Cook on high for another half hour.
6. Stir, and spread out on a wax paper-covered cookie sheet to cool.

Nutritional Info (¼ cup per serving):
Total calories: 229
Protein: 7
Carbs: 14
Fat: 18
Fiber: 4

Conclusion

When it comes to living a healthy life, what you eat is crucial. What you put in your body affects your brain, your heart, your skin...everything! If you are eating refined, processed, and packaged foods, you aren't getting the nutrients that your body needs. That means less energy, excess weight gain, and vulnerability to serious illnesses like cancer and diabetes. Luckily, it's possible to eat whole foods, which are untouched by artificial ingredients or stripped down. Whole-grains, organic produce, grass-fed dairy and meats, and more all provide your body with essential vitamins and minerals.

The slow cooker is a great way to prepare all your whole-food meals. As this book revealed, slow cookers are designed to cook just about anything at a low, slow temperature, so you don't have to babysit anything in the kitchen. You can start a meal in the morning, and by the late afternoon or evening, it's ready to serve. Even if you have a busy work life and little to no time to prepare homemade meals, the slow cooker can make it significantly easier.

This cookbook offered one hundred recipes to get you started, including breakfasts, beef, seafood, sauces, desserts, and even vegan food. You'll start to see similar ingredients pop up, so in the introductory chapters, you'll find a list of whole-food essentials that you should always have on hand. No matter what kind of budget you have or what your favorite types of food are, you'll find recipes that match your lifestyle and make healthy eating easier and delicious.

Thank you so much for reading this book!

I hope the book was able to teach you how slow cooking can simplify your everyday life.

Finally, if you enjoyed the book, then I'd like to ask you for a favor, would you be kind enough to leave a review for this book on Amazon? It'd be greatly appreciated!

I would love to give you a gift. Please visit happyhealthycookingonline.com to get these 4 amazing eBooks for free!

Made in the USA
Lexington, KY
30 December 2017